# PUBLIC INQUIRIES

Throughout the twentieth century, administrations have wrestled with allaying public concern over national disasters and social scandals. This book seeks to describe historically the use of public inquiries, and demonstrates why their methods continued to deploy until 1998 the ingrained habits of lawyers, particularly by issuing warning letters in order to safeguard witnesses who might be to blame. Under the influence of Lord Justice Salmon, the vital concern about systems and services allotted to social problems was relegated to the identification of individual blameworthiness. The book explains why the last inquiry under that system, into the events of 'Bloody Sunday' under Lord Saville's chairmanship, cost £200 million and took twelve and a half years (instead of two years). 'Never again', was the Government's muted cry as the method of investigating the public concern was eventually replaced by the Inquiries Act 2005, by common consent a good piece of legislation. The overriding principle of fairness to witnesses was confirmed by Parliament to those who are 'core participants' to the event, but with limited rights to participate. The public inquiry, the author asserts, is now publicly administered as a Commission of Inquiry, and is correctly regarded as a branch of public administration that focuses on the systemic question of what went wrong, as opposed to which individuals were to blame.

# Public Inquiries

## Wrong Route on Bloody Sunday

Sir Louis Blom-Cooper QC

•HART•

OXFORD • LONDON • NEW YORK • NEW DELHI • SYDNEY

HART PUBLISHING
Bloomsbury Publishing Plc
Kemp House, Chawley Park, Cumnor Hill, Oxford, OX2 9PH, UK

HART PUBLISHING, the Hart/Stag logo, BLOOMSBURY and the Diana logo are
trademarks of Bloomsbury Publishing Plc

First published in hardback, 2017
Paperback edition, 2019

© Sir Louis Blom-Cooper 2017

A catalogue record for this book is available from the British Library.

Library of Congress Cataloging-in-Publication data

Names: Blom-Cooper, Louis, 1926–author.

Title: Public inquiries : wrong route on Bloody Sunday / Sir Louis Blom-Cooper QC.

Description: Portland, Oregon : Hart Publishing, 2017. | Includes bibliographical references and index.

Identifiers: LCCN 2016049544 (print) | LCCN 2016049862 (ebook) | ISBN 9781509906789
(hardback) | ISBN 9781509906796 (Epub)

Subjects: LCSH: Governmental investigations—Great Britain. | Great Britain. Inquiries Act 2005. | Bloody
Sunday, Derry, Northern Ireland, 1972. | Massacres—Northern Ireland—Derry—History—20th century. |
Political violence—Northern Ireland—Derry—History—20th century. | Demonstrations—Northern Ireland—
Derry—History—20th century.

Classification: LCC KD4895 .B56 2017 (print) | LCC KD4895 (ebook) | DDC 342.41/041—dc23

LC record available at https://lccn.loc.gov/2016049544

ISBN: HB: 978-1-50990-678-9
PB: 978-1-50993-130-9
ePDF: 978-1-50990-680-2
ePub: 978-1-50990-679-6

Typeset by Compuscript Ltd, Shannon

To find out more about our authors and books visit www.hartpublishing.co.uk.
Here you will find extracts, author information, details of forthcoming events and
the option to sign up for our newsletters.

# PREAMBLE

When Sir Edward Heath spoke on 8 July 1982[1] in support of a House of Commons decision to review the actions of the Government leading up to the invasion by Argentina of the Falkland Islands, he said that 'the plain fact is that we have never succeeded in finding the perfect form of inquiry' into social scandals and national disasters, outwith the established courts of law. He was right. The methodology of the various inquiries—many of them by local authorities[2]—into matters of public concern (if they are entitled to a single rubric of 'public inquiry') has been unclear and messy. The mess was exemplified, inexplicably at the time of its outset in 1998, by the Bloody Sunday Inquiry, which, exasperatingly, took over 12½ years at a cost to the public purse of over £200 million. The book offers an overview of the history and function of public inquiries until the legislation of the Inquiries Act 2005 remedied the lack of clarity that was revealed in the Bloody Sunday inquiry in 1998 and thereafter. The legislative intervention of the 2005 Act hopefully answered the claim for abandoning any adversarial features of past inquiries (according to the Six Cardinal Principles of the Salmon Commission) and proclaimed the inquisitorial concept of a nascent administration of good government.

These are early days for the Inquiries Act 2005, but it has nevertheless already received almost full marks as a good piece of legislation. The House of Lords select committee in March 2014 in its post-legislative scrutiny said this:[3] 'the setting up and administration of inquiries … will make it easier to control both the length and cost of inquiries'. Revocation of Rules 13–15 of the Inquiry Rules 2006 'should alone cut months off the length of inquiries and reduce the cost proportionately'. A year later, in debate, the House of Lords endorsed those observations, heartily. It underlined the distinct phases of the procedure to be adopted, from the substantive task of evaluating the accumulated evidence, given those powers.

The burden of this book is to relate the scene of public inquiries over the last 80 years of the twentieth century and to describe generally how British governments had handled concerns of social scandal and public disaster, and how they were, often as not, mishandled in the various reports, both in their conduct and,

---

[1] Hansard HC vol 27 col 494. It was Edward Heath, as the Prime Minister of the day, who ten years earlier had appointed Lord Widgery to conduct the first Bloody Sunday inquiry.
[2] On 30 May 2016 the Government announced a review of the role and functions of Local Safeguarding Children's Boards, arising from the Wood report on inquiries into serious child abuse.
[3] *The Inquiries Act 2005: post-legislative scrutiny* HL Paper 143, para 297, p87.

more apparently, in their verdicts on social policy issues. The underlying cause of many inquiries was the insistence on replicating the habits of the lawyer in the courtroom (the advocate), underlined by the 1966 report of the Royal Commission on Tribunals of Inquiry (the Salmon Commission), which propounded the Six Cardinal Principles, endorsed in a government White Paper in 1973 (although, significantly, the Government did not follow it up with any legislation). Until then, the broad thrust of the various (and distinctly variable) types of inquiry reflected a governmental desire to reveal, unless specifically directed by the sponsoring minister, the reasons for the inquiry, and why and how the events under inquiry happened, sometimes with appropriate recommendations for change. It was a procedure that was distinctly inquisitorial in nature, decidedly not adversarial or litigious (most of the early cases covered matters of only minor concern), but was set up to assist ministers to obtain information, and in maintaining peace, order and good government. Only inferentially might the report of a public inquiry attach blameworthiness on the part of individuals if they were held to have acted culpably (or indeed, if their inaction had been culpable). The origin of the theme of investigation was that the public inquiry was always conducted inquisitorially, outside of the legal system, and that the panellists, even if serving or retiring judges, were commissioners of inquiry, not acting in their judicial capacity. They were tasked to act within the powers conferred on them by the terms of reference, with the procedural powers of the 1921 Act. The Commissioner of Inquiry did not don the wig and gown of a judge, even if that was his daily occupation.

The way in which public inquiries operated until the Inquiries Act 2005 is told through a series of cases from 1921 onwards. Broadly speaking, these inquiries were clearly differentiated from the disputes between parties to ordinary litigation by the procedural mode in which the inquiries were to be conducted. As Lord Scarman said in the Red Lion Inquiry in 1974, he was decidedly not conducting litigation, and hence the procedure to be followed was not adversarial. But all he would say, unhelpfully, was that the inquiry was 'to be conducted— and I stress it—by myself'. But how was the public inquiry to be described? Adversariality persisted.

The first section of the book (Part I) sets out the problems that public inquiries faced: the focus of inquiries on matters of procedure under the Tribunals of Inquiry (Evidence) Act 1921, with rare excursions into high policy issues, such as the Bank Rate Tribunal in 1957 and the Crown Agents case in 1982.

The second section (Part II) considers the government approach to the function and role of public inquiries. The watershed, as mentioned above, was the Salmon Report in 1966 and the Six Cardinal Principles it advocated. The leading textbook, Beer on *Public Inquiries*,[4] states that the Commission concluded that it is 'of the *highest* importance that these principles should *always* be *strictly* observed'. For two decades after the Salmon Commission, the dominant feature of the

---

[4] OUP, 2011, at 1.44 on p 16.

Salmon letter—the requirement to notify potential witnesses of any criticisms or allegations of blameworthiness—prevailed, akin to an indictment in criminal justice or particulars in a statement of claim. Invariably, public inquiries adopted the prescribed procedure of warning witnesses to safeguard their reputations. Indeed, in the Bloody Sunday Inquiry Lord Saville pronounced at the outset, at the opening hearing in July 1998, that the Salmon Commission's procedures and recommendations were not implemented by statute, and therefore not strictly law, 'but we recognised that it was as good as law'. Although that seemed to settle the role and function of public inquiries, it was certainly by no means the last word in the philosophy of public inquiries. The 'wrong turn' by Saville was to underline, even stress, the legal profession's claim to protect its separate clients against damage to their reputation (apart from legal responsibility) in the final report, as if they were facing a dispute with the State or its citizenry; often representation by their advocate in the conduct of the hearings did not promote the public interest, only the perception of their client. Additionally, Saville employed a private firm of solicitors to organise the arduous task of taking written statements from the witnesses who were to give oral evidence, an enhanced refinement of the process of issuing 'Salmon letters' to notify witnesses of alleged criticism before giving evidence.

This section of the book also argues that, despite the Bloody Sunday inquiry and the decision of Saville to follow the Salmon principles, the tide had, two years earlier, begun to turn against such legalism in the inquiry process. Even by the early 1990s, there occurred the decision of Lord Bingham in the Court of Appeal in 1993 in *Re Crampton*. That great judge (then Master of the Rolls) emphatically endorsed the methods of Ombudsmanry in a case involving the killings of children in Grantham Hospital by a nurse, Beverley Allitt. Lord Bingham said that the inquiry, set up by the Secretary of State, Virginia Bottomley, in 1993, should be held in private (witnesses were heard in private sessions and were not legally represented), rather than being a public inquiry with the full panoply of counsel for witnesses à la Salmon. It was pointedly chaired in the style of the Ombudsman system by a former holder of that office (Sir Cecil Clothier QC, an outstanding ex-Parliamentary Commissioner of Administration). Lord Bingham sounded a ringing endorsement to the public inquiry (in private and unrepresented) as an outcrop of public administration; he said, justifiably, that it was 'unlike any court of law'. (The Court of Appeal had dismissed the application for the judicial review challenging the minister's decision; the case is, surprisingly, unreported, and is not cited in the textbook by Jason Beer or his co-authors. The relevant parts are annexed herewith.)

The second event, from 1993 to 1996, was distinctly public, but without the presence of any legal representation at the oral hearings. The *Arms to Iraq* Inquiry was a non-statutory public inquiry conducted solely by Sir Richard Scott (later a Law Lord), supplemented only by his counsel, Presiley Baxendale QC, who had wide experience in public inquiries (and has been unjustly criticised for her limited role as questioning counsel). More important still, in Sir Richard's report of 1996, he emphatically rejected as unworkable the Six Cardinal Principles of the

Salmon Commission. The legal habit of confronting witnesses with counsel for other witnesses, as a prelude to oral testimony, was refuted and shown demonstrably to be flawed. (In several inquiries that I had conducted, the Salmon letter process had been disruptive in practice.)[5]

The *Arms to Iraq* Inquiry followed the collapse of prosecutions brought against arms dealers for unlawful trading of arms internationally, the Matrix Churchill case. The safeguards for witnesses in protecting their reputations evoked public debate, obscured by the ensuing Parliamentary challenge to Sir Richard's report in February 1997. The case also revealed the crucial culture of the judiciary in judicial proceedings, and the contrast between that and the role of civil servants in their duties to Parliament. The Conservative government won the ensuing motion in the House of Lords by a single vote; this signalled the need for a general governmental re-think on public inquiries. Hence, after the Labour victory in the General Election of May 1997, the urge to reform arose, strengthened by the growing delay thereafter in the report on Bloody Sunday. The Inquiries Act 2005, pronounced by a select committee of the House of Lords in 2014 as a good piece of legislation, was the result, subject only to the questionable power of warning witnesses of potential criticisms set out in the Inquiry Rules 2006.

By the mid-1990s the path towards a single statute to replace the 1921 Act was clear enough. The common law of England, apart from the purely procedural reforms of the 1921 Act, was developed in a number of cases in the Commonwealth countries of Australia, New Zealand and Canada, as well as Ireland. The Act of 1921 had been the last piece of legislation of the Imperial Parliament at Whitehall to become law in Eire. Unknowingly, apparently, to British politicians and practitioners, the Act had been taken over into Irish law as part of the partition of Ireland in 1922. Only one amendment, in the Dail in 1979, creating a power to the tribunal to award costs, was made by the Oireachtas. Nevertheless, the specific, legislated inheritance by Eire was the subject of detailed analysis of the Anglo-Irish system of commissions of inquiry in a series of cases in the 1990s, the most significant of which was the clearly-reasoned judgment of Mr Justice Murphy in *Lawlor v Flood* in 1999, which, above all, demonstrated that the 1921 Act did not entitle witnesses in public inquiries to be legally represented. This judgment reflected the classic expression of Mr Justice Brennan in the Australian High Court, that a public inquiry was 'sterile of legal effect'. A later chapter records the jurisprudence on public inquiries that might usefully have been included in the Bloody Sunday inquiry, including the *unreported* judgment of Lord Bingham in the case of Beverly Allitt. This authority and other cases went unrecorded, even unnoticed by Lord Saville.

---

[5] In the *Ashworth Hospital* inquiry, which I chaired in 1991–92, I warned against interpreting the Salmon letter procedure too rigidly, and suggested a formal review by the government. See Beer, *Public Inquiries*, 9.18 on p 359.

Part III (the Bloody Sunday section) examines in four chapters the egregious adherence to the Salmon principles in the Bloody Sunday Inquiry, ordered on 29 January 1998 by the Secretary of State for Northern Ireland in the Blair administration, allegedly preparatory as a feature of the Good Friday Agreement. It was the latest, and decisively the final fling of legalism as the mode of public inquiry, studiously to ascertain the events of 30 January 1972. Yet it took 12½ years to report. 'Never again' was the constant theme of political irritation and public opinion. While emphatically vindicating the 13 victims on the procession in Londonderry of any impropriety in exercising their civil rights to march (even though marching had effectively been banned by the Stormont administration) in protest at social injustices, the Inquiry's report and methods in June 2010 adhered obstinately (even expansively, and certainly expensively) to the legalistic Salmon principles, with its glaring omissions of public issues of systems and services related to public order. Lord Saville acted instinctively as a judge wielding judicial power; he leant heavily on Salmon legalism, with the inevitable consequence of a massive quantity of evidence of individual (instead of collective) action by 27 paratroopers of the British army, leading to an inquiry that cost more than £200 million.

The wrong road was hopelessly taken in two directions, all in the course of efficiency, which Lord Saville dubbed as 'thoroughness'. Not only did the Saville Inquiry give full sway to the concept of Salmon letters, discarded devastatingly by Sir Richard Scott two years previously in the *Arms to Iraq* Inquiry, but the Inquiry was also misdirected on its prime purpose, which should have been determining why and how the tragic event of 30 January 1972 occurred, rather than affixing blameworthiness on individual actors for the tragic events. In pursuance of 'thoroughness', contrary to the view in 1996 of the Council on Tribunals in its report at the request of the Lord Chancellor, Lord Mackay, which proffered instead the notion of 'effectiveness', Lord Saville firmly aimed to identify any (and if so, which) of the 27 individual paratroopers who, collectively, had indubitably killed the 13 unarmed victims. The multiplicity of oral evidence was hopelessly awry. It was not surprising that Lord Saville was unable to point exclusively to individual shootings.

Thus Lord Saville stumbled, and failed to find time to review the decisions of the military command in January 1972, in order to illustrate the circumstances that led up to the day of the civil rights march. In particular, he never dealt with the constitutional doctrine of military forces acting 'in aid of the civil power' that negated any prior consultation with the Londonderry police which initially favoured the holding of the march. Nor did he consider, let alone pursue in the courts, the availability to the military authorities of injunction proceedings against the organisers of the march, in the days before 30 January 1972. This omission, as well as other factors leading up to the civil rights march, should have been the main objective at the outset of the Inquiry. The failure to explain the genesis of the *soi-disant* 'arrest operation'—the crucial cause of the fatal shootings—beggars belief. The Saville Report also did not consider, supposedly for reason of lack of time, the other aspects of the background to General Ford's decision exceptionally to deploy the specialist company of paratroopers (not resident in the Province as part of the armed forces). No consideration was accorded to any agreement with the Londonderry police whether or how to perform 'an arrest operation' in conformity with the constitutional limit on the power of the Army to effect a civilian arrest. There is the additional aspect of the witness's memory of events, long since evaporated in time. The presumption must be that the Bloody Sunday Inquiry did not obliterate the lapse of time, although reliance was placed on the extensive media coverage of the day.

Part IV of the book explains how the growing distaste for the inordinate delay and cost of the Bloody Sunday Inquiry in the opening years of the twenty-first century prompted, even propelled, the Blair administration to effect a change that promoted expedition in public inquiries and even sought to control the output of public funds. It argues that the legislation that emerged, the Inquiries Act 2005, heeded the lessons of legalism in the inquiry process offered by Bloody Sunday, and has largely been successful in emphatically rejecting Salmon letters. Indeed, the proposed legislation had a clause that authorised the prospective chairmen to budget the exercise. This part of the draft was ultimately expunged in exchange for the provision of section 17(3) of the 2005 Act, imposing a duty of fairness in the conduct of the proceedings, intended primarily to instil in prospective chairmen a need to exercise control over the expected costs, and inferentially to limit the delay in reporting to the sponsoring minister.

The book concludes with the assessment of a good piece of legislation in the Inquiries Act 2005, subject to a proper revision of part of the Inquiry Rules 2006 (dealing with the safeguard of warnings to witnesses), at the behest of the House of Lords select committee in March 2014, and of a debate in the House in March 2015. So far, the Rules are unreformed. As explained in Chapter 12, the Chilcot Inquiry provided in a *Witness Protocol* that a witness facing any impending criticism in the final report was given an opportunity to respond to the imminent criticism. The result was a delay in the publication of that report, from October 2014 to July 2016.

There is a glance, peripherally, at Hillsborough (1989) and Litvinenko (2015) as models for public inquiries where the ministerial terms of reference specifically limited the scope of the inquiry. A look into the safeguards for witnesses at the reporting stage alludes also to the delayed publication of the Chilcot report. It all adds up to the structured future of commissions of inquiry.

Overall, the public inquiry under the 2005 Act is a part of the government's machinery for public administration. The theme is that the legalism of the Salmon Report, which dictated much of the practice of public inquiries in the second half of the twentieth century, is dead and buried. Devoid of any judicial power, the public inquiry conducted under the 2005 Act is a commission of inquiry. As such, its panellists are all commissioners of inquiry. Some might argue that public inquiries contain an element of judicial power, citing the practice of almost invariably appointing members of the judiciary to chair the inquiry. But that does no more than acknowledge the skills required in assessing the credibility and reliability of witnesses in the fact-finding process, which judges and trial lawyers possess in abundance. The 2005 statute merely requires the minister to ensure that his selected chairman has 'the necessary experience to undertake the inquiry' (the Inquiries Act 2005, section 8). But the aim of the legislation and practice of the 2005 Act is still not to import any judicial power, or indeed to introduce any aspect of the established legal system, unless ministerially limited in the specific terms of reference. A public inquiry is 'sterile of legal effect'; it shifts the burden from aping the litigious purpose of adversarial claims to the process of managing public concerns of mismanagement of governmental powers. It is an essential element of public administration.

# ACKNOWLEDGEMENTS

This book is the product of considerable involvement in the functioning of public inquiries from 1986–2004, as well as my acting (from December 2000–June 2004) on behalf of the Northern Ireland Civil Rights Association in the Bloody Sunday Inquiry. In the course of those activities, and in a study of the Inquiries Act 2005, I have had extensive meetings with those who have similarly been involved in public inquiries. Throughout these extensive discussions I have drawn on the help and information of a vast number of people, and not just my professional colleagues. It would be invidious to name them, large in number as they are. But I can at least thank them collectively for rendering me enormous help and, I hope, assisting me to avoid errors; whatever mistakes persist are entirely of my making.

I cannot, however, forbear one acknowledgment. Ian Aitkenhead has for the last decade been, part-time, my assistant in both researching relevant material and converting my script—some of which is barely legible—with superb excellence. His assistance has truly been invaluable, even immense in its quantity and quality.

# CONTENTS

## Part V: Final Thoughts

Part I

# Public Inquiries: Introduction

# 1

# Concern for Scandals and Disasters

The instinct to reach for the solution of a public inquiry stems from a desire to distract the critics or deflect criticism, or to expose some fraud, fault or act of maladministration. It also arises out of the need, expeditiously, to restore public confidence in government or in public administration, or to scotch ill-founded rumours of scandal, by an independent investigation of the events under scrutiny. The urge also is to establish the facts other than by established legal methods, such as coroners' inquests, litigation (including judicial review) or criminal proceedings. The problem of victims initiating class actions seeking legal remedies also prompts the call for of a public inquiry. The urge in government is to examine the relevant system and its services. It is not an alternative or additional method of determining any person's legal liability; civil or criminal liability is an issue exclusively for the courts of law.

Any hesitation there might be (and, not infrequently, is) officially to order such an investigation lies not so much in fear of the embarrassing exposure of misconduct or mismanagement by ministers or public officials, as in the sheer cost of such inquiries. Once established, there is little or no control (even by self-imposed restraint on the part of government) over the scope of the inquiry, or, consequentially, over the expenditure of public funds. How, for example, can one explain, let alone justify, the £6 million expended on the Clyde Inquiry into alleged child sex abuse in the Orkneys in 1992,[1] which did not even resolve the allegations of abuse, and served only to echo the failures of social workers and other agencies, so manifestly exposed by the Cleveland Inquiry three years earlier? And we have not heard the last of it. The instant review of the historiography of child abuse by the New Zealand judge, Lowell Goddard, which began in April 2015, lingers on. What indeed do we say of the Bloody Sunday Inquiry, lasting 12½ years at a cost of £200 million? 'Never again' has been the instinctive public cry. What is the explanation for taking an inordinate time to unravel the cause for public concern and to allay the public's confidence in the system and services?

---

[1] *The Report of the Inquiry into the removal of children from Orkney in February 1991*, 27 October 1992 (HC 195); *Report of the Inquiry into Child Abuse in Cleveland 1987*, July 1988 (Cm 412). See also, eg, *The Report of the Inquiry into Child Care Policies in Fife*, 27 October 1992 (HC 191). See also *Child Abuse: a Study of Inquiry Reports 1980–1989* (HMSO, 1991).

Apart from considerations of public cost, resort to inquisitorial techniques to expose the truth, contrary to, or at least in devaluation of entrenched due process rights, which are inherent in the adversarial system of justice, can be justified only if the purpose of the inquiry is kept firmly in mind. There is always a tension between the purpose of eliciting the truth and the protection of the individual against whom findings of culpability may have to be made. Two conditions must be satisfied. First, the inquisitorial process must not be directed or distracted by partisan advocacy; second, while the publicity engendered by public hearings and the final report may cause some harm and injustice to individuals whose conduct is brought under public scrutiny, fairness to the individual in the inquiry process, in the context of the public demand to know what happened and why, must be fully observed, but never overstated. Efficiency, rather than thoroughness, is the maxim, advocated by the Council on Tribunals in its advice solicited in 1996 by the Lord Chancellor. Private citizens may hope for, even expect, optimum protection; those who are public servants expect to undergo public scrutiny and accountability for their actions. The aim, understandably, is to reduce, if not eliminate, the tension in favour of the former. (Accountability is a modern concept that has developed generally in the field of judicial review.)

Given those two desiderata, what are, or should be, the functions served by public inquiries?

# The Aim of the Public Inquiry

There are four separate strands in the combined function of revealing the culmination of culpability or blameworthiness and the examination of strictures of public institutions and agencies. The four are: (1) to establish the facts; (2) to identify individuals' culpability; (3) to survey the arrangements that led to the scandal, disaster or abuse; and (4) to provide the symbolic purpose of holding up to obloquy the particular event that induced the crisis of public confidence. Strictly speaking, the inquiry's task is primarily, if not exclusively, to establish the facts so that action may be taken. Rarely, however, are an inquiry's terms of reference so restricted. However framed, they usually permit the inquiry to make recommendations, although ministers may properly regard policy issues as governmental matters not requiring the views of unelected delegates. Recommendations which suggest themselves to those engaged in the fact-finding exercise may, nevertheless, be valuable to policy-makers.

The problem of selecting the appropriate form for any inquiry is not without difficulties. The adversarial procedure adopted in the legal system, admirable as it may be for the resolution of defined issues in dispute between identifiable parties, is wholly inappropriate. It took some time for this to be recognised, with the legal profession addicted to its fondness for jury-like verdicts. There are, in a public inquiry, no immediately discernible issues to be tried according to well-established rules of evidence—although they may emerge in the course of the inquiry and may conceivably be reduced to definable issues. The ordinary process of civil litigation is neatly tailored to an adversarial, even a gladiatorial contest. The rules are framed to ensure a conspicuous even-handedness between rival disputants that, left to their own devices, may not actually promote the search for truth. Since the parties to litigation formulate their respective cases, call their own witnesses to support one party's case or refute the other party's case, and seek adjudication on the basis exclusively of such evidence, each party may seek to establish its own perceived version of the events. The result may be a satisfactory method for determining who should win or lose the forensic contest. But it does not specifically aim to establish an objective truth, still less to identify the relationship between that truth and a wider conception of the public interest. The public inquiry, on the other hand, is constructed—even instructed—precisely to elicit the truth. As Lord Justice Scarman stated in the Red Lion Square Inquiry in 1974, 'it is not litigation'. So what is it? It will ask itself: what happened; how did it happen; and who, if anybody, was responsible, culpably or otherwise, for it having happened. Any partisan view expressed in evidence should be relegated to assisting the overriding purpose. Is it now the chosen method of identifying and studying systems and those services that sustain them? And is the individual's blameworthiness relegated to an ancillary function?

Historically, the preferred method for establishing public inquiries was the Tribunal of Inquiry (Evidence) Act 1921. Before 1921 the practice had been to investigate alleged wrongdoings in public affairs through select committees of Parliament. There had been a recent revival of the select committee procedure to investigate issues which might otherwise be the subject of independent inquiries, or at least in addition to a public inquiry. The history of investigation by a political tribunal was, to say the least, unsatisfactory, if only because any parliamentary investigation induces partisanship on political lines; it lacks independent investigation. The Marconi scandal of 1912, which produced a division of view along strict party political lines—the majority exonerating ministers from all blame—rang the death knell of the public inquiry by parliamentary investigation. But the 1921 legislation, in establishing a procedure outside of, but authorised by, Parliament, gave the inquiry no more than the procedural powers of the High Court in adducing evidence and witnesses. The 1921 Act was passed, with a view to setting up some permanent machinery for investigating and probing into matters on the public agenda. The procedure under the Act was cumbersome. It provided that if both Houses of Parliament resolved that it was expedient that a tribunal be established for inquiring into a definite matter described in the resolution as of urgent public importance, a tribunal was appointed and had, for certain purposes, all the powers, rights and privileges vested in the High Court. The Act was an important step forward, from politically-conducted investigations to independent inquiries.[2] But it promoted the legal process.

The procedures employed by tribunals of inquiry under the Act, however, produced their own crop of profound dissatisfaction and led to the setting-up in 1964 of a Royal Commission under Lord Justice (later Lord) Salmon. That Commission suggested improvements by way of safeguards afforded to persons involved in the inquiries. The prime characteristic of the 1921 Act tribunals, underlined by the Salmon recommendations, was in effect to elbow out the inquisitorial aspect of public inquiries, in favour of procedural safeguards borrowed from the legal system. Indeed, the Salmon Commission (the Royal Commission on Tribunals of Inquiry) positively encouraged administrators and participants to turn the inquiry mainly into an accusatorial procedure: (a) by the framing of specific issues couched in the terms of reference; and (b) by conducting an adjudication of those issues by the methods familiar to English lawyers engaged in the court system. That, doubtless, was a satisfactory way of ascertaining the facts about specific issues, with legal representation to advance individual parties' cause, but it assumed always that these could be defined clearly at the outset (which is frequently not possible where issues may emerge only in the course of oral testimony, unrevealed by previously disclosed documentary material). It was hardly suited to most, if not all of the topics that were singled out for investigation by the 1921 Act procedure. Little use has been made of the 1921 Act in the last 45 years. In 1972 the Vehicle and General case, involving the supervision of an insurance company by ministers and civil servants, was investigated by a 1921 Act tribunal,[3] whereas the Barlow Clowes case in 1992 was left to the Parliamentary Commissioner for Administration to inquire into.

The virtual abandonment of the 1921 Act procedure, superseded in recent times by a bewildering variety of statutory and non-statutory inquiries under ministerial or local government aegis, each one adopting different techniques suitable to the topic under scrutiny, has not abandoned at least one major facet of the 1921 Act inquiries. It would not be overstating the case to say that many contemporary inquiries have been hijacked by lawyers, although social workers would argue, with some justification, that the legal profession has profited handsomely at the expense of social services in the large number of inquiries involving aspects of social work. Yet the adversarial features of the 1921 Act inquiries were maintained to the point where a fresh look at the system of public inquiries was called for. That is, until the Inquiries Act 2005 sought to resolve the legalism injected by the 1921

[2] The Aberfan landslide disaster, involving the National Coal Board, 1967; the leak of information about the Bank Rate in 1957; the Crichel Down case of 1954, inquired into by Sir Andrew Clarke QC, which was a manifestation of public concern over the manner in which government departments had handled a landowner's request to have his compulsorily-acquired land returned to him after the war, might have been suitable candidates for a 1921 Tribunal. Cmnd 3121.
[3] HC 133, February 1972.

Act, exposed by Sir Richard Scott in his report on Arms to Iraq in 1996. What form then should inquiries take?

## The New System of Public Inquiries

Section 2(1) of the Inquiries Act 2005 prohibits the inquiry in its report from finding or determining any person's criminal or civil liability, although it permits for an inference of legal liability to be drawn from its finding of facts; there is no inhibition to such objective inferences. The statutory prohibition is demonstratively an adjudication outside the established legal system. But is it intended to act as an auxiliary and legalistic method of litigation? If not, what kind of animal is it? Is it supplementary to the sole purpose? The terms of the Inquiries Act 2005 lean heavily towards a separate and distinct inquiry, emanating from and reporting to the administration of a government department or public authority. The question is whether the 2005 Act achieves the latter status without the legalistic input of professional representatives for the witness giving oral evidence to the inquiry. The pointer is the provision in the Act of 2005 of the requirement of 'fairness' throughout the conduct of the inquiry, and the methods of fairness enumerated in the Inquiry Rules 2006, particularly rules 13–15, which have been subjected to some criticism.[4] Fairness is the modern language that replaces, linguistically at least, the old concept of natural justice.

Apart from the statutory duty of the inquiry to conduct the proceedings fairly there is the prescribed caveat on the inquiry to ban anyone's blameworthiness. It may be inferred from the retelling of the fact-finding. Can we proclaim, then, that an ad hoc public inquiry is designed to expose the relevant system and its services; how did they function, and how can they be prevented? The reader's surmise is to favour an institution to disclose statutorily what the Common Law of England implicitly required, at least since the Tribunals of Inquiry (Evidence) Act 1921, and probably earlier in our governmental history. Does the Inquiries Act 2005 achieve that core purpose, and is it a reflection of public administration rather than a legal resolution? Has not the transformation in the Inquiries Act 2005 finally detached any public inquiry from its legal heritage? More accurately, they are, terminologically, commissions of inquiry as an outreach of public administration.

---

[4] See HL Deb 19 March 2015, vol 760, cols 1134–79.

# 2

# Early Beginnings: Corruption and Maladministration

It has taken a very long time—nearly 350 years—for Parliament to divest itself and its own members from conducting public inquiries, and instead invest the task in independent and impartial tribunals to undertake the analysis of social scandals and public disasters, punctuated by powers of procedure to adduce evidence and compel witnesses, as in ordinary legal proceedings. Under the Inquiries Act 2005 Parliament has sought to allocate the solution of a public concern about public systems and services to public administration in executive government. It replicates, for example, the development of the Parole Board from its inception as an advisory body in 1967 to an institution that combines its task of assessing the risk of criminality and its decision-making in respect of offenders with indeterminate sentences, while possessing no judicial power. Hitherto, there has lurked the claim of some kind of judicial aspect, a pronounced legalism within an inquiry system. Judiciality has now been replaced with public investigation of the events under scrutiny, a distinct shift from a legal process. The public inquiry now is 'unlike any court of law'.

Ever since 1679, when a select committee of the House of Commons was appointed to inquire into allegations that the Navy was riddled with agents of Popery, and that the Lord High Admiral, the Duke of York, had wantonly wasted public funds, the method of investigating the misconduct of public authorities was thereafter, until 1921, exclusively by the elected members of Parliament, or by a select committee of the House of Commons. The Tribunals of Inquiry (Evidence) Act 1921, which ostensibly replaced the parliamentary process with procedural powers, initiated the system for the rest of the twentieth century, until the disadvantages of the process were finally exposed by the system established by the Inquiries Act 2005. It prevailed until the debate initiated by Sir Richard Scott in the *Arms to Iraq* Inquiry in 1996 and a widespread discontent with the Saville Inquiry into Bloody Sunday over 12½ years (1998–2010). Apart from the nascent delay in investigation and the huge cost to the public purse, a subsequent study of its methodology reinforced the desire to implement reform of the public inquiry system.

The historical debate is frequently focused on the Marconi case of 1912–14 and is said to have inspired the legislation of the 1921 Act, establishing the independence of public inquiries. But, in effect, the Marconi scandal of 1912 was an isolated issue involving the standards of ministerial behaviour as well as allegations, later in the campaign, of governmental corruption. A typical formula, as expressed in the Marconi case, was composed of a select committee constituted along party lines in accordance with the proportion of parties in the House of Commons. In the Marconi case, of the 15 members of the select committee, six of them were Liberal members in the government of Mr Herbert Asquith (1908–16); other supporters in the majority on the select committee were drawn from the Irish party and Labour. Six were members of the Conservative Party, most of whom were legally qualified, including Lord Robert Cecil, QC, a prominent advocate at the Bar who did most of the examination of witnesses. The choice of serving members ostensibly endorsed a judicial approach to the task, but from the outset of the public inquiry the minority members from the Conservative Party actively prophesied that the select committee (with its majority of government supporters) would whitewash rather than reveal the truth of the events under inquiry. The predictable outcome was not one, but three separate reports together with a motion in the House of Commons which vindicated the ministers of any allegations of corruption. The six Conservatives produced their own report, supporting the allegations of corruption, and the chairman issued a third (conciliatory) report to achieve unanimity. None of them complied with the convention of a unanimous report; hence the myth of corruption was ultimately uncovered in the motion exonerating the Ministers, although the relevant evidence revealed attitudes towards the standards of behaviour in public concerning the belated disclosure of the acquisition of shareholding in the American Marconi company which had no formal links with its English counterpart. Two shareholders were Sir Rufus Isaacs, the Attorney-General, who was the relative of Godfrey Isaacs, the chief executive of the English Marconi company, and Lloyd George. No doubt the verdict, based inevitably on the majority membership, prompted the reform of the membership of select committees. The vote to support the government majority was, however, not just political ineptitude or manipulation; it was pre-ordained, and politically partisan.

The outcome of the Marconi scandal is often cited as the nadir of political control over the resulting report. But if that was an understandable reaction of the public, the abolition of the parliamentary resort to the select committee procedure did not emerge instantly. The onset of the First World War and other tribulations of Asquith's administration prevented early statutory intervention. Moreover, when reform came from the Bonar Law administration that succeeded in 1921, it entailed no provisions for the procedure to be adopted. The method of inquiry remained untouched, to be determined thereafter by the chairmen of post-1921 inquiries.

The long history of parliamentary inquisitions had been conducted from time to time in cases where there had been rumours in the media of lapses in standards of public administration and other related matters concerning the public good which demanded investigation to allay public anxiety. Because the ensuing inquiry (both in its institution and procedures) took the form of oral examination of witnesses by question and answer, the temptation (not to say the instinct) of members was to ape the scenario of the courtroom. The method of eliciting evidence, exacerbated by the cross-examination from Lord Robert Cecil, a doughty advocate as well as a prominent politician, lent the air of a court of law (often like a criminal trial) culminating in a report, judicially if not judiciously nuanced. The lawyerly habit died only belatedly. It remained pronounced in the last case under the 1921 Act, the Saville Inquiry on Bloody Sunday.

The Marconi scandal started out as a reminder of an unacceptable conferment by the relevant Minister (the Postmaster General, Herbert Samuel) of a project proffered by Godfrey Isaacs to extend Marconi's overwhelming expertise in wireless telegraphy to setting up stations throughout the British Empire. The allegations of corruption accumulated later in the foreign press as a result of hitherto undisclosed share dealings in Marconi shares in America. Allegations of insider dealing by certain ministers provided the necessary stimulus to hostile action by politicians, egged on by irresponsible newspapers.

There never was a scintilla of evidence to fault Herbert Samuel. As Postmaster General, he was responsible simply for arranging a contract with the Marconi company, which was at that time pre-eminent in the field of wireless telegraphy. As Roy Jenkins aptly described in his outstanding biography of Asquith,[1] the Conservative Party's pretence of a scandal was sustained only in order that anti-Semitic overtones of the affair might be exploited to the full:

> To bring together one Samuel and a couple of Isaacs in a skein of transactions bordering on high finance, was an irresistible attraction for [Hilaire] Belloc or Chesterton [Cecil, the brother of G K Chesterton, and editor of *The Tablet*; two prominent Anglo-Catholics].

The Marconi scandal may be (and often is) treated as a progenitor (or rather a political predecessor) to the modern system of public inquiries.[2] If so, it can safely be consigned historically to a single, unsubstantiated attempt to score publicly a political point over an opponent, with an unpleasant taint of racism. Not even a resort to the maxim, *post hoc, propter hoc*, supposedly evidencing cause and effect, can make it appear a respectable decision, or rescue a nasty affair in modern political and parliamentary history from drowning.

Whatever relevance the Marconi scandal may have for the political scientist, the case no doubt put an end to the exclusive use of parliamentary procedures to inquire into publicly untoward events. At least there would be no further committees, select or otherwise, to undertake the task. That much was evident, seven years later, on 21 February 1921. On that day, allegations were made in the House of Commons that certain officials at the Ministry of Munitions had been ordered to destroy documents relating to the entitlements of contractors, so that they would be paid more than they were entitled to receive. The matter was debated that evening, at which point the leader of the House, Mr Andrew Bonar Law (later Prime

---

[1] R Jenkins, *Asquith*, 2nd edn (Harper Collins, 1986), pp 250–51.
[2] See Beer, *Public Inquiries* (Oxford, Oxford University Press, 2011) paras 1.15–1.18, p 6, who claims that 'it was the unsatisfactory outcome that led to the replacement of Parliamentary Committees with public inquiries'.

Minister) proposed the setting up of a committee chaired by a judge, Sir Frederick Banbury. It was asked by the member for the City of London 'whether it would be necessary to have an Act of Parliament in order to enable the Committee which he is going to set up to take the evidence on oath'. After an exchange of views about a peremptory Bill to invest the tribunal with executive power, Mr Bonar Law replied: 'I will consult with the Attorney-General as to what differences there are in the way, and also as to whether it would not be possible to pass with the same facility a short general statute dealing with the matter'.[3] Thus was born the Tribunals of Inquiry (Evidence) Act 1921. The sole concern of the legislation was to replace the function of a select committee with a ministerially-appointed tribunal to confer the power to acquire evidence and witnesses on oath—a process to emulate the courts within the legal system eliciting evidence. The design of the intended legislation was that in the setting up by a Secretary of State, following a resolution of both Houses of Parliament into matters of 'urgent public importance', the tribunal was to have all the powers of the courts of law for compelling the production of documents, enforcing the attendance of witnesses, and examining them under oath. Inquiries would be set up by Parliament, a procedure abolished only in 2005. How they functioned evidentially and reported conclusions with or without recommendations, was a matter for the practitioners (mostly the legal profession).

Even before the 1921 Act, government departments had established public inquiries at which a leading lawyer was selected to chair the inquiry into the administration of local government and to report to the minister. There was no suggestion that a judge or QC's findings were invariably accepted. So too the assumption was assumed conventionally that in the case of an inquiry under the 1921 Act the chairman, even if a serving judge, was the chairman of a public inquiry. The inquiry's report was to the minister sponsoring it.

In July 1908 the Board of Education set up a statutory inquiry to investigate complaints against the local education authority by a Church of England school in Swansea. The choice of chairman for the inquiry was John Hamilton KC (later Lord Sumner, a Law Lord), then the Standing Counsel to the University of Oxford. Indeed, Hamilton's prominence was tantamount to a judgeship, to which he was appointed in 1909.

The Swansea school case arose out of Balfour's Education Act 1902. Ever since appearing on the statute book, the legislation had provoked intense indignation among members of the dissenting churches, and was taken up by the Liberal Party, opposition to the Act playing a part in the Liberal landslide of 1906. The Balfour Act sought to regularise the provision of elementary education in England and Wales, and to standardise the position of the non-denominational Board (or Council), subsidised from the rates, and the Church of England School, dependent on voluntary support, by placing both categories of school under the control of the local authority, which was put under a duty to allocate funds to both on

---

[3] HC Deb 22 February 1921, vol 138, cols 863–868.

an equal footing. It caused a reaction, especially in Wales, a Liberal stronghold, where Dissenters were in a majority and looked to the Liberal government to bring about the disestablishment of the Anglican Church in the Principality, where most schools were Church of England schools. The Dissenters complained that the Act discriminated against them, subjecting their children to Anglican doctrines and thus perpetrating the educational monopoly of the Church of England, at their expense as ratepayers. In turn they threatened to withhold payment of the rates.

It was against this background of bitter sectarian division, party political intention and parliamentary strife that the school in Swansea caused the kind of public concern that warranted a public inquiry, since in 1905 a complaint was lodged with the Board of Education that the Swansea education authority had flouted the law laid down in the Balfour Act by paying teachers at the Oxford Street Church of England elementary school at a lower rate than was being paid to teachers at the Board schools. In 1907 the cause became a public concern, when a conference of radical Welsh MPs, chaired by David Lloyd George (himself a Liberal government supporter and a pronounced opponent of the Balfour Act) passed a resolution in support of the local authority. The duty of the Commissioner of Inquiry, John Hamilton KC, was to examine the evidence, to ascertain the facts and to report his findings; he submitted his report at the end of September 1908 (after a two-day hearing). The facts were straightforward; the case was open-and-shut, the findings inevitable. The Commissioner held that the local education authority had manifestly discriminated against the Church of England schools. Experienced teachers had resigned in consequence; the rest were demoralised. The local authority was thus clearly in breach of its statutory duty 'to maintain and keep efficient' the school.[4]

Three months later, the Welsh department rejected the Commission's report out of hand. The Board of Education declined to accept either that the authority had failed in its duty, or that it had impaired the efficiency of the Church school by paying its teachers less. Astonishingly, the Board of Education upheld the action of the local authority. It simply overruled Hamilton's findings.

The repudiation of the report was denounced for what it undoubtedly was: a political manoeuvre designed to please sectarian opinion in a parliamentary constituency supportive of the ruling party (*The Times* of 17 February 1909 described it as a 'scandal'). The Board challenged the decision, which ultimately ascended to the Appellate Committee of the House of Lords. The Swansea affair continued to occupy both the media and Parliament. In time, Hamilton was made a High Court judge. His legal prowess ensured the promotion, despite the untoward publicity of the Swansea case.

The incident excited the legal profession over the Lord Chancellor's power to appoint political figures. But Hamilton's preferment was due solely to his high

---

[4] *Report of a public inquiry held under the Education Acts 1840–1907* by JA Hamilton KC (London, 1908); the report being issued as a Parliamentary Paper, Co 4542.

reputation at the Bar; he had not exhibited leanings towards the Liberal cause. The reverse was true; he became, as Lord Sumner, the last political Law Lord, but was quite independently a Tory supporter. The significance of the Swansea decision is more subtle. It reinforced the convention that the ministerial sponsor is fully entitled to reject the findings of a Commissioner, be he a judge or a senior lawyer.

Relentless litigation followed, which entirely restored Hamilton's findings. No one doubted, however, that the Board of Education was entitled to have regard to, or to disregard, Hamilton's clear report. It lost its case for rejecting Hamilton's findings, but only because it had acted quite unreasonably in its decision-making. It had clearly breached the bounds of its statutory powers, and *certiorari* was the legal outcome (an early predecessor of the judicial review of administrative action).

Giving reasons for an administrator's decision to overrule the report of a Commissioner is a requirement of a fair system of justice. In *Horada v Secretary of State for Communities and Local Government*[5] Lord Thomas of Cwmgiedd CJ observed that a proper and easy way to understand the explanation by the Secretary of State for rejecting the recommendation of a planning inspector in favour of market traders who opposed a planning development that would materially affect their trading was necessary. The Lord Chief Justice said that where the traders were put at risk and the inspector had given reasons on a matter of violent concern to the traders in a way that could be readily understood by them, the Secretary of State had to explain likewise his decision in the most readily understood way.

The use by experts advising the parties to an administrative decision of language understandable only to other experts and professionals was insufficient. They must give reasons for their disagreement with other experts, which means that they must express themselves in terms which can be understood in plain English. Those terms are inadequate unless they can be easily understood by the layman and not the intermediary of the lawyer or other professional adviser. The language of communication between the expert and the layman is crucial. So too the public is entitled to know, from Lord Saville's report, why General Ford opted for the method of an 'arrest operation' to combat the hooligans who were habitually desecrating the centre of Londonderry. They were told only that it was a military decision. But was it?

# The 1921 Legislation

The early history of inquiries under the 1921 statute disclosed a handful of cases which revealed rumours (often ill-founded) of suspected lapses in acceptable standards of public administration. Two of the fifteen titles of public inquiries

---

[5] *Horada v Secretary of State for Communities and Local Government* [2016] EWCA Civ 169.

over the first 40 years of the 1921 Act involved instances of leaked information; the one, in 1936, was the disclosure of the Budget; the other, in 1957, focused on the improper disclosure of information relating to bank rates. In both cases, the reports were designed to allay public anxieties about the quality of public administration. Only the loss in 1939 of the submarine Thetis on Merseyside evinced a national disaster. All other inquiries, until 1962, dealt with issues in the private sector, or otherwise outside the purview of the public sector. Thereafter, the emphasis on the issue of public inquiries took on a very different hue.

The Act of 1921 contained no provisions concerning the procedure to be followed by the tribunal; nor was there any provision indicating the mode of inquiry or as to the acquisition of evidence. Nor was there any provision that answers given to the tribunal by a witness could be used in any criminal or civil proceedings. Apart from the two inquiries in 1936 and 1957, the only important topic was the Lynskey tribunal of 1948 concerning bribery of ministers of the Crown or other public servants in connection with the grant of public licences. Typical of public concern at the time was the allegation in December 1957 that a boy in Thurso, Scotland, had been assaulted (a few cuffs over the ear) by two officers of the Caithness Police Force. If the case aroused any public interest in the UK, it hardly rated as the kind of instance that warrants the full panoply of the Scottish judiciary and legal profession. The chairman was a Court of Session judge, Lord Sorn. The tribunal's counsel was Jim Shaw (later distinguished in the House of Lords as Lord Kilbrandon). Other leading Queen's Counsel appeared for certain other parties. It was akin to using a sledgehammer to crack a walnut of minor public interest in the case of a wayward child. Why ever did it arouse such a response?

Some little interest was activated by public events in 1962 and 1963. At the close of the first day's play in 1962, the presiding Law Lord in the appeal in *Hedley Byrne Ltd v Heller* answered that he had that day accepted the invitation to head the inquiry into the circumstances in which the Official Secrets Act was breached by an Admiralty clerk, John Vassall. The case is notable for reasons directly and indirectly concerned with the tribunal's procedure and the public's perception of the allegations of spying by a public servant. Witnesses who appeared to be prejudicially affected by statements in the press or statements by the Treasury Counsel were informed of the allegations of blameworthiness which might be made against them. The tribunal was also notable in that, for the first time, the power to certify offences of contempt of court was invoked, and the public were excluded for security reasons from part of the proceedings. To compare the procedures to those of the ordinary courts of law, the 1921 Act gave the tribunal the like power to bring contempt proceedings. This power was invoked following the Vassell tribunal, when certain journalists refused to reveal the sources of their information.

127. The arguments in favour of the present provisions of the Act of 1921 are that it might be considered inappropriate that the Tribunal should commit as this would reflect adversely upon the impression that the Tribunal makes upon the public. It is inappropriate that an inquisitorial tribunal should have power to commit. The Act of 1921 was amended in the Committee stage to take the power to commit away from the Tribunal

and transfer it to the High Court, and this was for the protection of the individual. At that time, however, it was not known that chairmen of Tribunals would be persons holding high judicial office. The process of certification to the court and the procedural steps which have to be taken give opportunity for reflection by the Tribunal and the offender. The offender has the advantage of being dealt with by a court approaching the matter with a fresh mind. If the Tribunal had the power to commit, provision would have to be made for an appeal from its decision to the High Court. This would have the effect of making a decision of the Tribunal directly subject to appeal to the High Court— perhaps an undesirable precedent. The present procedure was followed in the Vassall Tribunal and proved to be procedurally satisfactory. There is a further complication that if the power to commit were vested in the Tribunal, the sentence of imprisonment might exceed the time during which the Tribunal would be in office and it is clearly preferable that the authority which commits should be in existence and approachable by the offender at any time during which he is serving his sentence.[6]

The other, indirect but significant, influence on the 1921 Act came extraneously to the re-hearing of the appeal in *Hedley Byrne Ltd v Heller*, which constitutes a landmark judgment in cases of professional negligence. The composition of the Appellate Committee was heavily weighted in favour of Chancery lawyers, with the presiding judge, Lord Radcliffe, himself a traditionalist lawyer. Counsel for the appellant company was seeking to reverse the Court of Appeal's majority judgment regarding the concept of a claim for negligent misstatements that could not be covered by contractual relationships, but by a relationship between the parties in which there was a duty of care implied. The unofficial plea to the Lord Chancellor was to appoint, in contrast, a court less reflective of the traditional equity lawyer. The postponed House of Lords, containing only one Chancery lawyer, found in favour of the claim, although in the instant case a contractual plea of exclusion from liability succeeded.

The following year, 1963, added fuel to the argument that the scope of public inquiries might usefully be tailored. Hitherto, there was an absence of intervention in matters of government administration by any institution other than the courts of law. The 1921 Act seemed to adhere to the principle that there was exceptionally a need for public inquiries as an auxiliary or ancillary to ordinary litigation. But by the late 1960s there was some disquiet at the solution of problems of public administration, uncovered by the 1921 legislation in matters beyond the maintenance of a code of behaviour by Ministers and civil servants. Public concern about such cases of maladministration was beginning to percolate the area of widespread scandals or disasters. One such event sufficed to stimulate a growing need for a wider review and, even, remedy. The Profumo case in 1963 was such an instance, even though the government of the day decided that to allay the widespread public concern an inquiry was necessary: but in what form? It decided, however, not to set up a tribunal under the 1921 Act; instead it appointed the Master of the Rolls, Lord Denning, to hold the inquiry. Ostensibly, the inquiry was

---

[6] *Report of the Salmon Commission*, para 127, pp 41–42.

a successful venture, despite the mode of conducting the inquiry being eccentric, if not even quixotic. It did at least repudiate any sense of a replication of normal standards of criminal and civil justice.

Lord Denning held his inquiry behind closed doors and interviewed witnesses without the presence of their lawyer. The witness heard none of the evidence against him or herself from other witnesses, and had no opportunity of testing such evidence. The transcript of the evidence has never been published, despite requests from interested parties to have a sight of what was said or not said. Lord Denning had in effect, so officialdom records, acted as detective, solicitor, counsel and judge. The Salmon Commission even had the temerity to describe it as achieving 'conspicuous success'. It said that:

> In spite of the many serious defects in the procedure, Lord Denning's report (Cmnd 2152) was generally accepted by the public. But this was only because of Lord Denning's rare qualities and high reputation as a brilliant exception to what would normally occur when an inquiry is carried out under such conditions.[7]

However the official conduct of the investigation of the public scandal was viewed, the mode of inquiry was never commended and remained an idiosyncratic (even aberrant) episode attributed to the individual judicial figure who is today perceived retrospectively as a judicial misfit in the history of the legal system in the twentieth century. But if the Profumo report is now treated as an antiquity in reacting to public concern for scandals and disasters, it is an incident of the system that began (or did not then begin, but was at best in embryo) the questioning of what to do in the inquiry system. It was certainly a time for official review, which came soon enough.

---

[7] para 21, p 15.

# Part II

# The Principles of Public Inquiries

# 3

# The Royal Commission on Tribunals of Inquiry 1966 (the Salmon Commission)

The Home Secretary of the day, Mr Roy Jenkins, on 28 February 1966 appointed seven members, under the chairmanship of Lord Justice Salmon (a Lord Justice of Appeal and later a Law Lord), 'to review the working of the Tribunals of Inquiry (Evidence) Act 1921, and to consider whether it should be retained or replaced by some other procedure; and if retained whether any changes are necessary or desirable; and to make recommendations'. The Commission's remit was distinctly procedural. It was not asked to consider what form a public inquiry should take. It said:

> 4. (a) The evidence that we have received has shown that the criticisms of the working of the Act of 1921 were not such as to call for its replacement by some other procedure. We have however recommended certain alterations in the present procedure to improve its efficiency and particularly to safeguard persons called to give evidence before Tribunals and also persons who may otherwise be interested in the subject matter of the inquiry. *Some of these alterations will involve legislation.*[1]

The alterations were not statutorily enacted. The government endorsed the Committee's recommendations, including the Six Cardinal Principles, in 1973, but did not achieve legislation; nevertheless, their influence dominated for the next 30 years.

The composition of the Salmon Commission indicated its focus. It was dominated by the legal profession; only two members (Viscount Stuart and Wilfred Heywood) were not legally qualified. The others favoured academically-inclined lawyers. Arnold (later Lord) Goodman was an established solicitor and political 'fixer' for the Labour administration of Harold Wilson. John Butterworth was a legally-qualified university administrator (an early vice-chancellor of Warwick University). Professor H W Wade was the distinguished holder of a chair at

---

[1] Italics supplied.

Cambridge in public constitutional law and administrative law. The final member was Mr Dick Taverne who resigned from the Commission on 7 April 1966 (only weeks after appointment) to become the Joint Parliamentary Secretary of State to the Home Secretary.

It is not intended to question the reliability nor the quality of expertise to review the procedures for public inquiries. The Committee appeared simply to emphasise the legalistic approach. Its importance was in favouring the traditional habits of the established legal profession towards the protection of individual actors in public affairs that prompted public disquiet as to their performance in national scandals or disasters. Such a high-powered membership might have had profound views as to the role and function of public inquiries, in the course of which they would have enunciated the existing and future place of such social events in the administration of a modern democratic government, expounding its constitutional status. That it did not—and could not properly do so—was evident from its specific terms of reference. Its report resoundingly reflected that limited course of action. It is odd that Lord Saville at the outset of the Bloody Sunday Inquiry should have stated so authoritatively that although the Salmon Commission was not made law, it is regarded as establishing the law. It never purported to do more than increase legal procedure in the investigations.

To enhance the tribunal's task of collecting the evidence required for its inquisitorial function (as opposed to the adversarial procedure employed in courts of law), the Commission members insisted forcibly on the habits of the English accusatorial system; in essence, witnesses who might be criticised for their conduct had to be allowed professional representation and the ability to refute (if they needed to do so) the specific manner in which they had conducted themselves. The result was the Six Cardinal Principles.[2]

30. There are important distinctions between inquisitorial procedure and the procedure in an ordinary civil or criminal case. It is inherent in the inquisitorial procedure that there is no *lis*. The Tribunal directs the inquiry and the witnesses are necessarily the Tribunal's witnesses. There is no plaintiff or defendant, no prosecutor or accused; there are no pleadings defining issues to be tried, no charges, indictments, or depositions. The inquiry may take a fresh turn at any moment. It is therefore difficult for

[2] 1. Before any person becomes involved in an inquiry, the Tribunal must be satisfied that there are circumstances which affect him and which the Tribunal proposes to investigate.

2. Before any person who is involved in an inquiry is called as a witness, he should be informed of any allegations which are made against him and the substance of the evidence in support of them.

3. (a) He should be given an adequate opportunity of preparing his case and of being assisted by his legal advisers. (b) His legal expenses should normally be met out of public funds.

4. He should have the opportunity of being examined by his own solicitor or counsel and of stating his case in public at the inquiry.

5. Any material witness he wishes called at the inquiry should, if reasonably practicable, be heard.

6. He should have the opportunity of testing by cross-examination conducted by his own solicitor or counsel any evidence which may affect him.

persons involved to know in advance of the hearing what allegations may be made against them.

The Salmon Commission opined, however, that the difficulties and injustice with which persons involved in an inquiry may be faced can be largely removed by following scrupulously the Six Cardinal Principles.

These qualifications on the application of an inquisitorial procedure were avidly adopted by the management of public inquiries (including other statutory and extra-statutory provisions) as endorsed by the Government's response to the Salmon principles in 1973.

# Salmon Letters to the Fore

The Salmon Report in 1966 said that it was of the highest importance that its Six Cardinal Principles should always be strictly observed; it concluded that the 1921 Act should be amended so that anyone called as a witness would have the right to be legally represented. While accepting the Six Principles and their expression, reflected in the issuance of 'Salmon letters' to alert witnesses to allegations of fault on their actions or inactions, the Government's view, tardily some years later, was that they should be used as guidelines. It qualified the guidance commended so forcefully by the Royal Commission as operative 'in circumstances in which certain of the principles will be capable of being observed in the spirit and not in the letter'. Above all, the government accepted the recommendation that anyone called as a witness should have the right to be legally represented. Significantly, only 'considerations of public cost should not be allowed to prejudice the decision'. The right to legal representation should be qualified by a discretion in the tribunal to ascertain and prescribe the particular issues in which the applicant for representation is an interested person.

Even though the Six Cardinal Principles were never made statutorily enforceable, the forcefulness of their status in the Report had the practical effect of religious-like observance of their desirability in practice. They were avidly seized upon by the legal profession as a conventional method of safeguarding the witness. Thus, the dominant feature of Salmon letters, which so aped the dictates of the litigious process of the legal system, took hold of the public inquiry scene. The Salmon Report dealt with the procedure for public inquiries rather than misconceiving their primary purpose.

Stripped of the minutiae of procedural problems that permeated public inquiries before 1973, the Six Cardinal Principles became the bible of public inquiries for the next 30 years; all those engaging in public inquiries adopted the procedure that ultimately exposed the flaw in simply replicating the principle of the legal system in giving the optimum opportunity to a witness to answer potential blame for his actions or omissions.

# Their Demise

Thus, until the Six Cardinal Principles were exposed to trenchant criticism by Sir Richard Scott in his *Arms to Iraq* Inquiry in 1996, the tenor, and the inevitable time taken in revealing their exposition by the elaborate process of examination and cross-examination of their individual clients by advocates, public inquiries became dominated by the legal profession, in what I described as an unwelcome and unhelpful infusion of adversarial techniques. There was no doubt that the 'risks of hurt and injustice [which] are inherent in, and cannot be eliminated from, any procedure which is effective for arriving at the truth' was a stumbling block to a full implementation of the legal right of witnesses to legal representation. Advocates in the courtroom are not readily controllable by the tribunal! One mordant commentator said, after reviewing the Saville Inquiry on Bloody Sunday, that it was as if the system of public inquiries had been hijacked by the legal profession, through its insistence on the legal principle of witness representation. But witnesses are not parties to public inquiries.

There is still a yearning for the Six Cardinal Principles. In the House of Lords debate on 19 March 2015,[3] Lord Brown of Eaton-under-Heywood argued that 'the Salmon principles themselves are essentially sound'. But, in the context of public inquiries, is this yearning realistic? The statute in 2005 (as discussed below) omits any requirement of a warning of criticism to a witness before he or she gives oral evidence, save that any special need to forewarn a witness is encompassed by the overall requirement of the inquiry to act fairly throughout. That apart, it is now realistic to infer that Salmon letters are largely a matter of history, buried by the rejection of the legalism of the Salmon recommendations.

Sir Richard Scott, in his 1996 report, rightly observed that the Six Cardinal Principles carried strong overtones of adversarial litigation. It was a gentle reminder that, over the three decades since the report of the Salmon Commission, successive public inquiries (both statutory and non-statutory) had adopted the process in the issuing of Salmon letters, by at least singling out potential defaulters of their duties. In setting out the Six Principles *in extenso*, Sir Richard affirmed that the purpose of a public inquiry was primarily to identify the relevant systems and services. Only as a secondary consideration should the inquiry indulge in determining blameworthiness.

Sir Richard's insistence on the fundamental aspect of fairness throughout the conduct of the public inquiry was evident. At the same time he was ever mindful of the flexibility of the inquiry system which, from time to time, might exceptionally provide for the cross-examination of a particularly susceptible witness. But, in summary, the procedure he advocated was politely directed at the legal profession which had assumed so rigorously the right (even constitutionally enforced) of

---

[3] HL Deb 19 March 2015, vol 760, col 1159.

legal representation for the witness who desired to protect himself or herself from the inherent prejudice of their conduct in the inquired event. And Sir Richard warned that there might still be occasions which should not hamper unnecessary involvement of adversarial principles. He alluded to the techniques of advocates whose duty to their clients may be used to deflect the inquiry from its perceived task, or even indulge in delaying or obfuscating tactics.

Sir Richard, in considering Salmon letters and other aspects of the legal system, kindly quoted something I had written questioning the presence of legal practitioners in fora that dissociated their purpose from ordinary litigation.[4] He wrote, approvingly:

> Sir Louis Blom-Cooper has commented that 'The prime characteristic of the 1921 Act tribunals, underlined by the Salmon recommendations, was in effect to elbow out the inquisitorial aspects of public inquiries in favour of procedural safeguards borrowed from the legal system', and that '...the Salmon Commission ... positively encouraged administrators and participants to turn the inquiry into an accusatorial procedure (a) by the framing of specific issues couched in the terms of reference and (b) by conducting an adjudication of those issues by the methods familiar to English lawyers engaged in the court system'.

---

[4] My article on 'Public Inquiries' can be found at (1993) 46 *Current Legal Problems* 204.

# 4

# The Jurisprudence of Public Inquiries

Apart from a contempt case in the High Court in 1962 against two journalists reporting on the Vassall tribunal[1] and two, exclusively procedural, aspects in the Bloody Sunday Inquiry which ended up in the Court of Appeal,[2] there is an astonishing absence of any case law defining the justification and philosophy of public inquiries generally, or under the Tribunals of Inquiry (Evidence) Act 1921. Even more astonishingly, there is no reference in English appellate courts (final or intermediate) to an array of decisions of appellate courts of the Commonwealth and from the Supreme Court of Ireland. Our comparative blindness to Anglo-Saxon and informative material in this area of public law is puzzling. Those views from abroad are instructive in indicating the speciality of public inquiries as offshoots of public administration, and decidedly not part of the adversarial system of civil and criminal liability. The explanation may be that the absence of a written constitution in England precluded any such debate; after all, the 1921 Act was unarguably procedural in its scope; it did not allude to the role of a public inquiry. As Sir Thomas Bingham MR (later Lord Bingham) noted in *Crampton v Secretary of State for Health*,[3] procedures suitable for inter-party litigation or criminal procedure are by no means appropriate for a fact-finding exercise intended to result in management recommendations.

Before 1999, there had been several decisions in the courts of the British Commonwealth, and in Ireland. It is instructive, however, to recall two statements in the 1980s from the High Court of Australia, in considering the functions and role of commissioners of inquiry. In *Victoria v Australian Building Construction and Building Labourers' Federation*,[4] a Royal Commission inquired into unlawful behaviour of a trade union or its members. Mr Justice Stephen stated:

> The appointment of a commissioner to inquire into and report upon the commission of a crime creates no prerogative criminal court; his report can neither commit anyone nor

---

[1] *Attorney-General v Mulholland and Foster* [1963] 2 QB 477. In *Lord Saville of Newdigate v Harnden* (2003) NI 239 the Court of Appeal in Northern Ireland dismissed Lord Saville's appeal to find a *Daily Telegraph* journalist in contempt of court for refusing to give the Inquiry his sources, on the grounds that he had no obligation to reveal the source of the information supplied to him.

[2] *R v Lord Saville, ex p A* [1999] EWCA Civ 3012; *Lord Saville v Widgery Soldiers* [2001] EWCA Civ 2048.

[3] *Crampton v Secretary of State for Health* (9 July 1993, unreported).

[4] *Victoria v Australian Building Construction and Building Labourers' Federation* (1982) 152 CLR 25.

involve those consequences which a curial finding of guilt entails. The only direct consequence of his reported conclusion that a particular person committed a crime is that the
mind of the Executive is informed in that conclusion.

That could be said to be the genesis of the restriction on a public inquiry not to
find or determine civil or criminal liability, as is now declared in section 2(1) of
the Inquiries Act 2005. At pp 152–153 Mr Justice Brennan spoke more widely on
the question of legal liabilities:

> A commission of mere inquiry and report—affecting no rights, privileges, or immuni-
> ties, imposing no liabilities, exposing no legal disadvantage—cannot be (unless the cir-
> cumstances are exceptional) either an authority for the assumption of judicial functions
> or an interference with the judicial process. Even if a commissioner be directed into and
> report upon a contravention of the law, the inquiry and report are *sterile of legal effect*
> [italics supplied].

And he added, pointedly:

> It is not the nature of the facts to be found but the legal effect of the finding which may
> stamp an inquiry as judicial ... The absence of any legal effect in the findings of a royal
> commissioner appointed merely to inquire and report denies any suggestion that such a
> commissioner is exercising judicial power.

Irish courts have followed suit. It is highly significant that the Tribunals of Inquiry
(Evidence) Act 1921 was the last enactment of the Imperial Parliament at Whitehall
to be written into the law of the Republic of Ireland in 1922. The constitutionality
(or rather its absence) was amply considered by the Supreme Court of Ireland in
*Haughey v Moriarty*.[5] The Chief Justice, Hamilton CJ, delivering the judgment of
five Justices,[6] dealt extensively with the 1921 Act (as amended in 1979 by adding
the power of a Commission of Inquiry to award costs) having regard to the provisions of the Irish constitution. That statutory change by the Dail might still have
impacted on Lord Saville's approach to the funding of a public inquiry. But it did
not, unhappily.

The Supreme Court repeated and concurred with the statement made by
Costello J in *Goodman International and Laurence Goodman v Hamilton (No 1)*:[7]

> There is no statutory provision which empowers the establishment of the tribunal
> either by the two Houses or the Minister. *It is established by an administrative act,* [italics
> supplied] that is by order of the Minister of the 31st May 1991.

And he added, from the judgment of Costello J:

> The Minister can inquire into matters of public interest as part of the exercise of his
> executive powers, but if this is done without reference to Parliament then the inquiry will

---

[5] *Haughey v Moriarty* [1999] 3 IR 1, following *R v Haughey* [1971] IR 217, involving a different
individual, Padraic Haughey.
[6] Denham J (now the Chief Justice), Barrington J, Keane J (later to become Chief Justice) and
Murphy J were the other four.
[7] *Goodman International and Laurence Goodman v Hamilton (No 1)* [1992] 2 IR 542, 554.

not have statutory powers which are to be found in the Tribunals of Inquiry (Evidence) Act and the Tribunals of Inquiry (Evidence) (Amendment) Act 1979.

Only the government or any minister can inquire into matters of urgent public importance as part of their executive powers. And Hamilton CJ added that the presumption of constitutionality which has been afforded by the court to Acts of the Oireachtas 'extends neither to pre-1922 Acts of the later United Kingdom Parliament nor to [Ireland's] pre-1937 legislation'.

In endorsing the judgment of Geoghegan J at first instance, the Supreme Court found that the activities of the tribunal of inquiry fulfil virtually none of the fundamental conditions or characteristics of the administration of justice. Even if, by reason of the inquisitorial nature of the tribunal, it is not accurate to speak of a controversy concerning the violation of the law, the proceedings could not conceivably make the proceedings of the tribunal an administration of justice within the meaning of the Constitution. In short, the process of the public inquiry lacks any judicial power: it is 'sterile of legal effect'.

This is not to suggest for one moment that a party to adversarial proceedings has extensive natural rights and that a witness before a tribunal has none. It is merely to recognise that the need for rights in determinative proceedings differs from those which have no such consequence and that some of the rights long associated with adversarial proceedings do not translate into those of an inquisitorial nature.

The detailed consequence of a public inquiry was exemplified in the judgment of Mr Justice Murphy, in the course of his assenting judgment in *Lawlor v Flood*,[8] apropos the status of witnesses.[9]

Irish authorities were significantly considered by Lord Justice Girvan in *Re Walker*.[10] When the case was decided on 15 December 2008, it made specific reference to cases from the Irish Supreme Court, most relevantly to the judgment of Mr Justice Murphy in *Lawlor v Flood*. He noted, however, the existence of constitutional issues that are fundamental in the Irish constitution, but omitted to observe the view of Hamilton CJ.[11]

At the outset of the application for judicial review by the Chief Constable of the Police Service for Northern Ireland and Steven Walker, challenging two procedural rulings of June 2008 in the Rosemary Nelson inquiry, Lord Justice Girvan[12] observed that in considering the Irish constitution he had to read the Irish cases in their constitutional context, and that he had himself drawn these authorities to the attention of the parties 'and relisted the matter for further argument'. On the two procedural issues, which the English courts had held were eminently for

---

[8] *Lawlor v Flood* [1999] IESC 67.
[9] The passage is quoted in Chapter 5 herein, pp 45–46.
[10] *Re Walker* [2008] NIQB 145.
[11] Quoted above.
[12] At paras 16 and 20.

any public inquiry to determine, Girvan LJ concluded, 'not without hesitation, that this court should not interfere with the Inquiry's decision on this aspect of its ruling'. Perhaps the novel position in the Inquiries Act 2005, allowing for 'core participants' to be legally represented (even with its limitation on the form of such representation), meets the extent of a claim for safeguards for witnesses.

What, then, was the initial approach to the appropriate function of the public inquiry, conducted specifically under the authority of the 1921 Act? The question demanded a clear answer. At the preliminary hearing on 21 July 1998, Lord Saville said: 'if you look at the Salmon Report which has not the force of law—I think everyone accepts it as representing the law'. Thereafter Lord Saville made no allusion to the cases (mainly in Australia, Canada and the Republic of Ireland) that might have persuaded him to take a different road in the Bloody Sunday Inquiry, nor indeed was the view of Brennan J in the Australian High Court, that tribunals were 'sterile of legal effect', cited. He made no reference to the criticism made of the Salmon Commission by Sir Richard Scott in 1996 in the *Arms to Iraq* Inquiry (a non-statutory inquiry), where he cast considerable doubt on the application of the Six Cardinal Principles which had hitherto been scrupulously adopted in a variety of public inquiries. More specifically, he endorsed the Six Cardinal Principles of the Salmon Report that set out the safeguards for witnesses who might be criticised and embellished them by employing a private firm of solicitors (at an estimated cost of £6 million) to organise written statements from all the witnesses in conjunction with consulting the witnesses' legal representatives. This was Lord Saville's demonstration of 'thoroughness' in the Inquiry's task.

Everything thereafter flowed inevitably from an adherence to an adversarial process, save only that there was an explicit acknowledgment of the prohibition in finding or determining any civil or criminal liability, which were matters exclusively for the traditional legal system. Inferentially, the Saville Inquiry took a stance on the task that was distinctly akin to those methods habitually preferred by lawyers in litigation.

The trenchant remarks made in the judgment of Mr Justice Hardiman (prematurely deceased in 2016 at the age of 57) in the Supreme Court of Ireland as recently as 21 April 2010 in *Murphy v Flood* are highly pertinent today.[13] He said:

> I wish urgently to recommend to those responsible for the establishment of tribunals a book "Illinois Justice" by Kenneth A. Manaster (University of Chicago Press, 2001). This is an account of an inquiry presided over by the future U.S. Supreme Court Justice John Paul Stevens into suspected bribery by banking interests of Justices of the Illinois Supreme Court. The inquiry began in mid-June 1969 and was over by the end of July 1969. Stevens announced the terminal date before he began his work. He insisted on the narrowest possible terms of reference. He brooked no extension of them. The cost of his six week inquiry was a miniscule fraction of any of our tribunals. In his foreword

---

[13] *Murphy v Flood* [2010] 3 IR 136.

to Manaster's book, Justice Stevens contrasts this speed and economy with the "Special Counsel" inquiries subsequently established in the United States. Yet none of the latter, to my knowledge, have extended to anything like as long as the present Tribunal.

Before the legislation of 2005 there was precious little by way of overseeship by the courts of individual reports of public inquiries. That there was *no* appellate system was axiomatic, but did it preclude any judicial monitoring? While there was a steady stream of judicial pronouncements within the courts of the Commonwealth, there was no judicial review in England until the Bloody Sunday Inquiry. During the protracted hearings of those proceedings—in July 1999 and December 2001—the Inquiry by the Saville tribunal was judicially reviewed in order to challenge certain procedural orders of the tribunal, on the subject of the anonymity of retired and serving soldiers and the appropriate venue for the giving of their oral evidence. Until then, judicial control over the practice and procedure of public inquiries had not emerged in the UK courts. Both judicial reviews, which went to the Court of Appeal, had serious cost implications that might conceivably have been saved; in both, the result was adverse to the tribunal's claim that it had the authority exclusively to control its own procedure. Both cases proceeded to endorse the approach initiated by Lord Saville jurisdictionally, and both acknowledged that the chairman conducts the proceedings discretionally, but otherwise judicially reviewable. In Irish terms, the Inquiry had no constitutional status: it was simply an administrative act of government.

Part III

# Bloody Sunday; Second Time Around
# 1998–2010

# 5

## The Wrong Turn in 1998: A Final
## Dose of Inappropriate Legalism

The Bloody Sunday Inquiry (the second public inquiry into the tragic event in Derry on 30 January 1972) was established on 29 January 1998. The last words spoken in the public hearings took place on 28 November 2004, with the closing submissions of counsel to the tribunal, Christopher Clarke QC (now Lord Justice Christopher Clarke). Between those two dates, over 445 days of oral sessions, the tribunal heard 450 civilian witnesses and 150 military personnel and other individuals concerned with the policing and the aftermath of the march organised by the Northern Ireland Civil Rights Association. The first inquiry by Lord Widgery in 1972 took only 11 weeks, from 1 February to 11 April, and exonerated the paratroopers (with one minor exception) from any legal liability or other blameworthiness. On 23 September 2009 Lord Saville announced that the report would be delivered to Downing Street on 22 March 2010. It finally reported on 10 June 2010, after 12½ years. The cost to the public has been estimated at about £200 million.

## Introduction

It was positively *not* the task—at least not the primary concern—of the Saville Inquiry to conduct an exercise akin to establishing precise findings (not civil or criminal liability) to identify the shootings of 13 civil rights marchers by a proportion of 27 individual paratroopers acting in concert in pursuance of a military command, a *soi-disant* 'arrest operation'. But that was the main, even overriding effect of the protracted hearings over six years. Lord Saville marginalised (even distorted timeously) the essential aim of this public inquiry, which under general and unspecific terms of reference (not substantially altered from those set out in 1972 for Lord Widgery)[1] was principally to find out what happened on that day,

---

[1] The Tribunal's terms of reference were to inquire into: 'the events of Sunday, 30th January 1972 which led to loss of life in connection with the procession in Londonderry on that day, taking account of any new information relevant to events on that day' (the last 12 words were only added to the terms of reference in 1998).

why it happened, and to recommend any changes to the relevant system and services. The most relevant aspect to the day was the 'arrest operation', which was to be effected only at the conclusion of the civil rights march, after three hours of an orderly procession. The policing of the march preceded it, and tactically promoted the entry of the paratroopers on to the scene of the tragedy. That was the direct cause of the tragic shooting, over a period of a quarter of an hour on a sunny afternoon on the streets of Londonderry.

It was unquestionably obvious from the outset of Lord Saville's inquiry that the fatal shots had come from the paratroopers' rifles, no matter which particular paratrooper fired the fatal shot that killed which particular victim. At an early stage the tribunal itself acknowledged that 'after all, [this] is an inquiry into events in which people lost their lives and were wounded by British army gunfire on the streets of a city in the United Kingdom'.[2] It would have been simpler and much less extensive and costly if Lord Saville had started from the assumption of a collective responsibility of the paratroopers for the killings and put aside for the moment any question (if justified) of individual blameworthiness in the separate paratroopers who filed the fatal shots. Once the inquiry was embarked upon with the single (perhaps ambiguous) exercise of 'establishing the truth', all else followed, including a 12½ year wait until the report. In unbalancing the aims of a public inquiry (not a rehearing of the Widgery whitewash of 1972) the circumstances leading up to and surrounding the Inquiry relegated the primary aim of a public inquiry. The purpose of a public inquiry is to determine how the disaster happened; why it came about; and to make recommendations to review and reform the system and services. *In essence, the method of inquiry chosen by Lord Saville was intellectually flawed.* The vindication of the marchers in the ultimate verdict in June 2010 was much less impressive than it seemed to the public. The vindication of the victims (the reversal of Lord Widgery's findings) and a denunciation of the paratroopers were vital, but they were subsidiary to the main purpose of the public inquiry, to find out why and how the tragic events happened.

The Saville Report adhered to the traditional (mistaken) approach of 1921 Act inquiries, adopting the Six Cardinal Principles of the Salmon Commission. It is not without interest to note that the decision by the Court of Appeal in reversing the decision of the Saville Tribunal and granting the paratroopers the right to give their evidence anonymously was on the basis that such a right should be granted to them collectively. The anonymity of each of them which 'the tribunal could be expected to have in the forefront of its mind' was relevant to the danger stemming from their individual names being revealed.[3] Lord Saville's insistent use of the word 'thoroughness', as a prerequisite of his methodology, was his starting

---

[2] Lord Woolf MR cited this passage in *R v Saville and others* [1999] EWCA Civ 3012 at para 55.
[3] See para 60 of Lord Woolf's judgment.

point in the overall aim of obtaining the truth. Truth is multi-faceted; it is always institutionalised by the context of its specific functioning. The primary object of the inquiry was, as the Court of Appeal observed, 'getting at the truth of what happened', the happening being the shooting by a company of paratroopers. The truth of the event focused upon was, in part only, the fatal shooting by soldiers; it mattered not one wit which soldier fired his rifle. The soldiers acted as a unitary force, and that force killed the 13 victims. The precise identity of the killers, and indeed their victims, was basically irrelevant to the truth of what happened.

At the preliminary hearing on 21 July 1998 Lord Saville said, '... if you look at the Salmon report which has not the force of law—I think everyone accepts it representing the law'.

Thereafter, Saville never doubted the validity of the Six Cardinal Principles, so palpably viewed as flawed by Sir Richard Scott only a couple of years earlier. He never alluded publicly to the assault upon their validity in Scott's 1996 report in the *Arms to Iraq* Inquiry or the ensuing public debate. And there was no reference to the jurisprudence on the substantive law, reflected in the Irish and other cases in the 1990s.[4]

In his ruling on 24 July 1998, he stated that the correct basis on which to proceed was stated in the Royal Commission Report on Tribunals of Inquiry of 1966. Lord Justice Salmon had explained the difference with the ordinary civil and criminal proceedings that the recommendation sought to implement. The Saville Inquiry, however, went further and embellished the application of Salmon letters to be delivered to a witness who might be criticised; the inquiry indulged in a wide range of legal representation for interested parties, endorsing the principle in the Salmon Report that witnesses interested in the event should be forensically safeguarded against alleged criticism, and he employed a firm of solicitors to undertake the production of each witness statement. Thoroughness, Saville asserted, demanded that each shooting of a victim had to be examined and analysed. Nothing could be more telling than in the representation which Lord Saville gave to the one of the 27 paratroopers against whom there was special suspicion. In addition to the collective representation of the military, he gave single representation of one leading counsel, junior counsel and solicitors for Private L.

In hugely amplifying a procedural method of conducting public inquiries in the mould of the Salmon safeguards to potential witnesses, the Saville Inquiry, by implication, rejected the forthright attack on the Salmon Six Principles made by Sir Richard Scott in his 1996 report of the *Arms to Iraq* tribunal. The Scott Inquiry on *Arms to Iraq*, held between 1993 and 1996, dispensed entirely with legal representation for witnesses. All the questioning was conducted by Sir Richard himself and his counsel, Ms Presily Baxendale.

---

[4] See Chapter 4.

# Causality; The Scope of Culpability

The focus on the cause and effect of the killing of the 13 victims and the shooting by the paratroopers of the British Army was inevitably distorted; it presented future difficulties. As Lord Saville stated at the preliminary hearing on 24 July 1998, 'We are very disappointed that to date very few of the soldiers present in Derry on Bloody Sunday have been identified, let alone located'.

The problem of acquiring statements from individual paratroopers continued throughout the investigation to hamper the aim of the Inquiry to acquire evidence of the shootings by individual paratroopers. The tribunal laboured on, in the hope that concerted efforts would produce the witnesses to the shootings. At this early stage of the lengthy inquiry there had been an opportunity to take stock of the task referred to the Inquiry, and to consider the possibility of delay. None was envisaged, although there were intervals during the years of hearings (1999–2004).

When Lord Saville was confronted in January 1998 with the prospective conduct of the Bloody Sunday Inquiry, he and his legal team had the immediate problem of determining how the tribunal under the Tribunals of Inquiry (Evidence) Act 1921 should set about the daunting task of unravelling what occurred on the fateful day in January 1972 when 13 innocent citizens at the end of a civil rights march in the city of Derry were shot at and killed by a company of paratroopers of the British Army, imported exclusively to support the policing of the march, in execution of an 'arrest operation' which had been devised by the military commander, Sir Robert Ford. The tribunal's terms of reference were precisely those given to Lord Widgery in February 1972—'to inquire into the events of 30 January 1972 which led to the loss of life in connection with the procession in Londonderry on that day'—save that Lord Saville's terms of reference added the phrase, 'taking account of any information relevant to the events of that day'. There was no hint of a break between the march and the immediate aftermath of the 'arrest operation'. No marcher could be the object of arrest until the conclusion of the march.

Lord Widgery's finding in his report on 11 April 1972 exonerated, almost totally, the paratroopers from any culpability for the killings. The report was widely regarded sceptically. Almost everyone in the context of Northern Ireland, who could be described as unbiased, concluded that the report was a whitewash.[5] Their scepticism has been fully justified, 40 years later. There had been no question, in 1972, of conducting an appeal against Lord Widgery's report which had been astonishingly expeditious; from beginning to end it took only 11 weeks. But the evident public dissatisfaction (which grew increasingly and variously, both over the intervening years and during the protracted tribunal proceedings from 1998–2009) with Lord Widgery's 'whitewash' of the military action led inexorably to Saville distinctly distancing his inquiry from the previous inquiry. A fresh start

---

[5] Drewry, 'Judges and Political Inquiries: Harnessing a Myth' (1974) 23 *Political Studies* 49, 59.

was justifiably called for. But at the very least the shootings were shown to have come from the paratroopers. The issue which Lord Widgery purported to resolve was whether these shootings were justifiable homicides by the military under orders (Saville's report revokes that justification).

Apart from receiving approximately 2,500 witness statements, the Inquiry compiled 33 bundles of evidence comprising about 160 volumes, including 13 volumes of photographs. The estimate is that these bundles were composed of 20–30 million words. The evidence was recorded electronically, and was sent in CD-ROM format to the interested parties. Hence, the enormity of the task which the Inquiry set itself to perform. No isolated issues were to be resolved: no predefined questions of fact had to be answered; and no question about the criminality or serious misconduct of anyone was mentioned for determination.

The choice of chairman to head the Inquiry was important—not so much for the person chosen for the task, as for the selection of the individual from among the holders of high judicial office. Given the political inclination to select a member of the judiciary (which itself has come to be regarded as a dubious practice wherever the investigation is politically sensitive)[6] the sponsoring minister was bound to follow the precedent of the appointment of Lord Widgery in February 1972, who was then Lord Chief Justice of England and Wales.

Lord Saville, a Lord of Appeal in Ordinary, had spent a professional career in the practice of commercial law, displaying a pronounced intellectual talent and a penchant for information technology that was manifest in the equipment used by the Inquiry for instant transparency of documentary material and online transmission. Those attributes rendered his appointment attractive, while at the same time infusing a sense that his disposition to approach the task was essentially from a distinctly lawyerly viewpoint. Elsewhere there is the thought-process of a legal mind, as opposed to that of an administrator devoting a flexibility that focuses on the context of the factual event under inquiry. That naturally favoured the process of fact-finding in the mode of the courtroom. Even though the Inquiry was properly and consistently acknowledged to be inquisitorial, and dissociated itself from the traditional evidence-gathering of the litigious process, the legalism of the adversarial mode of civil or criminal trial was ever-present—the elaborate preparation of written statements from potential witnesses, prepared by professional lawyers contracted out by the Inquiry team; the oral examination of witnesses by counsel to the Inquiry; cross-examination by counsel for interested parties[7] (although Lord Saville, wisely, was at pains to emphasise that cross-examination was not permitted before his Inquiry, and insisted that it be referred to as questioning and cross-questioning—it seemed a distinction without a difference); and constant legal submissions by counsel, resulting in applications to the courts for

---

[6] Professor J Beatson, Lionel Cohen Lecture 2004, as reported in 37 *Israel Law Review* 238.
[7] Restrained, not always successfully, by the chairman insistent on forestalling unnecessary or unhelpful repetition of detailed points.

judicial review on two procedural aspects of the Inquiry—the anonymity of soldier witnesses and the venue for the oral evidence of former soldiers.

Overall, the ethos of the Inquiry was barely distinguishable from the tenor of forensic proceedings, save for the overriding feature that the scope of the Inquiry was dictated, not by parties in definable dispute, but by the aims of the Inquiry. The process adopted by the Inquiry and governed only by its ample terms of reference chimed perfectly with the innate desire to demonstrate thoroughness in its perceived task. Thoroughness was, *par excellence*, the watchword of the Inquiry. It was in the event performed diligently, to the nth degree. Was that, however, the right, or indeed the only strategy to adopt in order to comply with the public interest or 'matter of public importance' (to use the terms of the statute), as demanded by the terms of reference? Lord Saville had forewarned his audience:

> We are proposing to gather together everything of relevance, to publish everything of relevance to the world, let alone to those who are interested in this room; and then to call oral evidence and to subject it to our cross-examination in an attempt to reach the truth. Whatever the rights and wrongs of Widgery, none of that happened there. People were not given the sort of opportunity we are going to give them now to sit back for months and look at this material.[8]

Thoroughness, translated into practicality by a principled decision-maker, might at the outset have been dictated by two distinct approaches to compliance with the terms of reference:

1. As a discrete and crucial element in the overall requirement to investigate the events on Bloody Sunday, to ascertain whether victim A (unarmed and engaged in a civil rights march) was killed from a bullet fired from soldier X's rifle;[9] or
2. To assume that the death of the 13 victims was the result of direct military action (as distinct from the policing of the march) against the victims, without determining precisely how each one of the 13 had been killed, which soldier had been directly responsible for firing the fatal shot, assuming a collective responsibility on the part of the paratroopers, under military command to fulfil the 'arrest operation' designed by the GOC (NI), a lesser imposition than findings of individual criminality or serious misconduct by the soldiers.

Lord Saville instinctively chose the former stance. The latter approach (in addition to the practical difficulties of adducing the evidence) would have substantially reduced the time and effort in asking each individual paratrooper about the precise use of his rifle that killed a particular victim, or indeed the examination of the rifles. It should have been greatly preferred, and would not have undermined any formal proceedings after the Inquiry report. It would, incidentally, have negated

---

[8] Preliminary hearing transcript from 20 July 1998, p 49.
[9] This does not refer to Soldier X, who was one of the witnesses at the Inquiry.

the law's injunction not to intrude upon any legal liability, other than inferentially from the process of fact-finding.

Lord Saville opted decisively, and unprompted by any other approach to thoroughness, for the first alternative. In relation to the matters raised at the preliminary hearing, that approach had already been set in train, and Lord Saville did not appear to countenance any other view. No discussion about the task set by the terms of reference took place at the preliminary hearing on 20 and 21 July 1998. (It is interesting to note that the precise terms of reference do not appear to have been discussed with Lord Saville. In the *Arms for Iraq* Inquiry conducted by Sir Richard Scott, such a discussion took place before the terms of reference were finally announced by the Prime Minister on 16 November 1992.)[10] Public satisfaction, it might be asserted, could be accommodated by nothing less than that high degree of 'thoroughness'. What did the Minister include in 'the events' of 30 January 1972?

There is always a gap between the cold print of an inquiry's terms of reference and the tribunal's translation of them into action. Three factors filled the gap in 1998: a) the legal aspects of a 1921 Act tribunal of public inquiry; b) a lapse of 30 years that distinguished—evidentially, at least—the task of Lord Saville from that of Lord Widgery; and c) the cost of the Inquiry. These factors should have determined, at the outset of the Inquiry, the proper approach to its terms of reference. Was it necessary to engage in such an expensive exercise?

Little wonder then that the media commentator and the public servant alike should instinctively proclaim that such an inquiry should 'never again' be undertaken. It was an ill-directed inquiry. Thirteen innocent victims were fatally shot by paratroopers of the British army, fleeing from gunfire; it was established that the thirteen had not provoked any military reaction by the paratroopers, or indeed those policing the march (except for a minor disturbance at barrier 14, early on the march. Yet a study of the role and function of the Saville Inquiry in January 1998, and consistently thereafter, reveals at most, to overwhelming public satisfaction, the vindication of the unarmed deceased citizens, but also resulted in the protracted, predictable reversal of the whitewash of the first inquiry 30 years earlier, which came from 11 weeks of elucidation by Lord Widgery. In one sense the latter excursion was unique. Not only was there a fresh re-run of the evidence on the day, but subsequent reportage was also admitted. The inquiry was more aptly an investigation. The massive inquiry by Lord Saville unravelled the topic by way of a traditional form of inquiry. It vouchsafed an adherence to the judge's perceived duty of thoroughness. It embarked on what had formerly been seen as a predictable processing of a scandal, until Sir Richard Scott's questioning of the appropriate procedure for inquiries in the *Arms to Iraq* Inquiry. That contentious event, which eclipsed the erstwhile legal procedure, also revealed that the aim of public inquiries was to expose the system and services of any impugned event.

---

[10] See *Report of the Inquiry into the Export of Defence Equipment and Dual-Use Goods to Iraq and Related Prosecutions* (The Scott Report) HC Deb 15 February 1996, vol 271, cols 1139–64.

Blameworthiness of individuals in the process of services and social systems was to be relegated to an ancillary function, in decreeing, in the Inquiries Act 2005, that there should be no capacity to find or determine, other than inferentially, the civil or criminal liability of anyone involved in the scandal or disaster. Lord Saville's explanation, if not excuse, is a stubborn act epitomising the unreformed legalism in public inquiries over the twentieth century. But if Lord Saville adopted, unquestioningly, the legal profession's habit in its unique mode of inquiry, he did not overcome the inherent fallibility of the traditional approach. Time and the ensuing costs never entered into the perceived duty to investigate the facts in full measure. It was a classic instance of one of the more damaging phrases in the English language—'we have always done it this way'.

# Two Inquiries, 40 Years Apart—An Overview in Scope and Cost—the Concept of Memory

Lord Widgery (appointed Lord Chief Justice of England and Wales in 1971) had instantly accepted the invitation by Sir Edward Heath to conduct an inquiry on his own, and reported on 11 April 1972 that paratroopers of the British Army had shot and killed 13 marchers on the streets of Derry on 30 January 1972. His bold, even preconditioned (or perhaps preconceived) report concluded that the Northern Ireland Civil Rights Association (which did not give evidence at the inquiry, although it submitted evidence of the march) was to blame for having organised and managed the march banned by the government at Stormont, and that the paratroopers, with one minor exception, were exonerated of any responsibility for the tragic deaths of 13 innocent victims. Whatever conclusion can be drawn from the report, it is clear that it did not allay any public doubt. Hence the re-run of 29 January 1998 in the context of the Good Friday Agreement of that year.

Nearly 40 years later, Lord Saville (a serving Law Lord) revived the hotly-contested finding of Lord Widgery and found that the killings were demonstrably unlawful. He declared that NICRA and the marchers (including specifically the 13 victims) were entirely innocent of any wrongdoing, except for defiance of the governmental ban on marches in the Province which had come into effect on 9 August 1971. That finding was warmly commended (itself commendably) by the Prime Minister in a statement that day (15 June 2010) in the House of Commons. The Prime Minister, in acceptance of the report (exemplified by language of conspicuous candour) said that 'it is right to pursue the truth with vigour and thoroughness, but let me reassure the House that there will be no more open-ended and costly inquiries into the past'. In his finding that the marchers were vindicated of any blame for the deaths, Lord Saville expressly held that each of the victims was shot and killed by the 27 paratroopers who were individually examined and cross-examined before the Inquiry in hearings ending in October 2004.

Lord Widgery's terms of reference had been to report on the circumstances pertaining to the deaths incurred as a result of events at the march. He amplified the procedure recommended by Lord Justice Salmon in 1966, which was commended officially only afterwards, in the government response of 1973. Precisely the same terms of reference were given to Lord Saville on 29 January 1998, as a prelude to the Good Friday Agreement of April 1998, except additionally Lord Saville and his two Commonwealth judicial members of the panel were told that they could properly consider in their report any additional evidence that emerged after the event. Much of that was contained in a vast amount of journalistic (radio and TV) material recorded by the media, which had flocked in huge numbers to survey the operation of the march, policed sensibly by the resident battalions of the British Army. Journalistic witnesses gave oral testimony of what they saw and heard, as well as subsequent interviews of actors from the day's events. The journalistic outpourings then and subsequently uniquely served to support any findings of fact by an independent tribunal.

Apart from the critical finding by Lord Saville in June 2010, that vindicated the marchers of any wrongdoing and held the paratroopers (and their commanding officer) blameworthy, the second public inquiry's remit called for an investigation of a number of other issues, primarily to deal with the system of policing the civil rights march and the services deployed to that end. Tacked on to the end of the march was the 'arrest operation', to be effected by the paratroopers. These and other procedural problems are commented upon marginally in the extensive report of 5,000 pages, and are covered in this chapter. Over and above the overwhelming finding in favour of the marchers, too few of the issues raised in the Inquiry (indeed some of them dismissively on the ground of inadmissibility for the Inquiry) were covered. They are dealt with elsewhere, but the major comment focuses on the approach made by Lord Saville to the evidence of individual shootings by the paratroopers.

# What Next?

Any public inquiry, whether statutory or non-statutory (before or after the 1921 Act), is quintessentially an aspect of public administration. It is decidedly not a process of civil or criminal justice conducted in a court of law, governed by rules of evidence and litigious procedures.[11] Indeed, it is quite unlike anything entrusted to a court of law, as Lord Bingham stated in 1993.[12] The minister, who is responsible for everything that occurs (or may occur) within the province of his or her

[11] Lord Scarman's opening statement at the Red Lion Square Inquiry in 1974 has become a classic source of tone and format for the inquisitorial procedures of a major public inquiry. See Sedley, 'Public Inquiries: A Cure or a Disease?' (1989) 52 *MLR* 469, 470, fn 3.

[12] *Crampton v Secretary of State for Health*, unreported.

ministry, occasionally faces an issue of public concern that needs full investigation. For reasons of the scope and nature of the issue, as well as to indicate impartial and independent investigation, the minister is unable sensibly to satisfy the public interest by an internal inquiry. He needs to be fully informed about the event. Civil servants are demonstrably not independent, even if they are not ostensibly partial; the overriding need is to seek outside help to conduct the public investigation. The ensuing inquiry is therefore essentially the long arm of the minister; he or she sets out the inquiry's terms of reference that provide the parameter of the inquiry. Ideally, the terms of reference should at the outset be agreed with the prospective chairman (as they were in the *Arms to Iraq* Inquiry), thus avoiding any ambiguity that might evoke a challenge by way of judicial review. By the terms of reference, the minister indicates precisely what it is he wants to be investigated: no more, no less. Unlike litigation, the determiner of the investigation is the minister, and not any of the parties in dispute as between themselves. The minister's concern is the public interest—to ask how the issue arose, why it arose, and how it can be avoided in the future. The tribunal reports its findings to the minister, and may make recommendations. Nothing it says binds anybody. And there is no appellate structure; only the Inquiry's mode of operation is judicially reviewable. Even publication is a matter for the minister, although nowadays that is almost always automatic. But it is the minister who is exclusively responsible for publication, although it may be announced in advance that the report will be published. It is the chairman's duty to make the report to the minister and not to publish the report in advance of ministerial action.

The clear distinction between the public inquiry and any form of litigation or dispute resolution is the fundamental rule that the inquiry must not determine or render a verdict of anybody's civil or criminal liability, although the inquiry body may infer some blameworthiness in the course of its fact-finding exercise. The prohibition on civil and criminal liability was almost certainly the basic principle of the law after the abolition in 1640 of the Star Chamber.[13] A leading case in the Canadian Supreme Court[14] said this:

> A Commission of Inquiry is not a court or tribunal and has no authority to determine legal liability; it does not necessarily follow the same laws of evidence or procedures that a court or tribunal would observe. A Commissioner accordingly should endeavour to avoid setting out conclusions that are couched in the specific language of criminal culpability or civil liability for the public perception may be that specific findings of criminal or civil liability have been made.

Mr Justice Hardiman of the Irish Supreme Court in *O'Callaghan v Mahon* added,[15] '[it] merely reports its opinions and makes recommendations. It does not

---

[13] See Mummery, ibid, pp 292–301.
[14] *Canada (Commission of Inquiry on the Blood System)* [1997] 3 SCR 440.
[15] *O'Callaghan v Mahon* [2006] IR 32 at 74.

make binding findings of fact, though its report can, of course, have the effect of vindicating some persons and utterly destroying the reputations of others.' Is that enough reason for the blamed as well as 'the others' to be legally represented? I think not. It is a fate of public exposure. The primary, even the overriding, purpose of a public inquiry is not to apportion blameworthiness on anybody, unless to illustrate the reasons why the issues inquired into are explicable only by reference to human action or inaction. Those are matters exclusively for courts of law.

# Witnesses

If judges are appropriate commissioners of inquiry, dissociated from their judicial functions in the legal system, what, if any, should be the function of other interested parties in the process of the enquiry, the potential witnesses to the events under inquiry? The position was neatly stated by Mr Justice Murphy in the Irish Supreme Court in *Lawlor v Flood*:[16]

> The purpose of a public inquiry, such as the present is twofold: first, for the Oireachtas [the Irish Parliament] to obtain information to enable it to perform more effectively its legislative functions and secondly, to assuage public concern as to the existence of a particular state of affairs. The second of these purposes manifestly requires that the business of the Tribunal should be conducted in public. That general requirement is tempered by the limited statutory exemption in favour of private sittings. This exemption is necessary to avoid giving undue and privileged publicity to wholly unsustainable allegations and it is desirable also to ensure that the Tribunal equips itself with adequate information to conduct a meaningful public inquiry. However, the fact that the sole member and [the chairman's] counsel or advisors will have a body of information available to them would not of itself convert the inquisitorial proceedings into one of an adversarial nature.

> Clearly an inquiry *may* ... evolve into a charge by the investigative body against what should be a witness. On the other hand, it is to my mind, inconceivable that witnesses who are called before a Tribunal to give such evidence as is available to them in relation to the subject matter of the Tribunal should be treated as defendants in civil or criminal proceedings or afforded the rights which would be available to such parties. An inquiry as such does not constitute legal proceedings (whether civil or criminal) against any person: less still does it constitute a multiplicity of legal proceedings against each and every of the witnesses subpoenaed to appear before it. If such were the case it would be impossible to conduct any inquiry. In that event it would be necessary for each witness to cross-examine not only the witnesses who gave evidence before he did but also that he should have an opportunity of cross-examining those who gave evidence after he had been heard.

---

[16] *Lawlor v Flood* [1999] IESC 67.

Nobody, least of all interested parties (including potential witnesses) has any rights to protect; at most they may have their reputations at stake. Mr Justice Murphy went on to deal with the position of witnesses who are interested parties:

> It must be remembered that the report of the Tribunal whilst it may be critical and highly critical of the conduct of a person or persons who give evidence before it is not determinative of their rights. The report is not even a stage in a process by which such rights are determined. The conclusions of the Tribunal will not be evidence either conclusive or *prima facie* of the facts found by the Tribunal.

> This is not to suggest for one moment that a party to adversarial proceedings has extensive natural and constitutional rights and that a witness before a Tribunal has none. It is merely to recognise that the need for rights in determinative proceedings differs from those which have no such consequence and that some of the rights long associated with adversarial proceedings do not translate into those of an inquisitorial nature.

Consistent with that exposition of the status of witnesses before an inquiry, not possessed with rights and only variable interests, there have been instances recently where inquiries have dispensed with any direct participation of legal representatives in the inquiry process. But the active participation of legal representatives in the eliciting of evidence from witnesses called to give oral testimony was resolved. The legislation of 2005 has at least limited the scope of legal representation of any interested party (as determined by the chairman in his/her discretion) to 'core participants'—a terminological change to move inquiries away from connotations of litigation. Indeed they underlined legal representation to a limited class of interested parties. There is little doubt that the legal profession over the years had taken full advantage of full-blown advocacy in the style of the criminal or civil court. Subject only to some necessary control of the scope of any cross-examination of witnesses by the chairman of the Inquiry, much time and cost to the public purse was taken up with the conduct of the proceedings by advocates for the interested parties. Some of the desire to limit the length of proceedings through lawyer-participation was prompted by the protracted proceedings of the Saville Inquiry into Bloody Sunday, but it was not sufficiently effective. Costs and delay in public inquiries were, over many years, the source of acute public attention and not a little sense of public scandal. The Saville Inquiry palpably provoked reform, and it will manifestly never be repeated. But it religiously followed the traditional pattern functioning since 1966, which had been discredited in 1993–96 when Sir Richard Scott broke the ice of legal professional dominance. Has the 2005 Act now done enough to solve the basic problem of the costs and time spent on a procedure that emulated, if not replicated, the litigious process? It is necessary to examine the general conduct of the Bloody Sunday Inquiry, to ascertain the persistent defects of the traditional attitude to public inquiries.

Not until there was access to the 5,000-page report of the Bloody Sunday Inquiry, and an opportunity to study its vast contents, was it possible to determine the *leitmotif* of Lord Saville's Inquiry: the 60-page summary issued on the day of publication of the report was quite inadequate to judge the scope of Lord Saville's interpretation of his terms of reference and their implementation, although the massive evidential material indicated the scope of the Inquiry. The unravelling of that question was ultimately revealing, and prompted expert critique.

The focus of that day that ended in tragedy was, not unnaturally, the short period of time on the streets of Derry when the shootings occurred, together with detailed consideration of the events immediately preceding the entry of the paratroopers onto the scene, to effect 'the arrest operation' against perceived rioters at the end of the march, which, as the indirect cause of the fatal shootings, is described later. This focus led the Inquiry, emphatically and rightly, to vindicate the 13 victims of any wrongdoing whatsoever, such as might conceivably justify the military's unlawful killings. For the rest of the events leading up to the deployment of the paratroopers on that day, the report—with one notable exception—is proportionately minimal, even scanty, in its treatment of issues relevant to the public inquiry's primary task of finding out why and how the tragedy of the day evolved.

Lord Saville, forthrightly, rejected all the conspiracy theories levelled at members of the Cabinet of Sir Edward Heath, which had been a staple diet of Irish republican rhetoric for the last three decades, accentuated by the widespread fury generated by the exoneration of the military in Lord Widgery's report of 11 April 1972. But even the most ardent commentators of the Irish troubles among the nationalist writers have been arguing that it was wrong to stop the allocation of blameworthiness with a finding of disobedience on the part of Colonel Wilford to a military order from Brigade HQ, as Lord Saville did, and go no higher in the military hierarchy—except, of course, for consigning conspiracy theories to the forensic dustbin.[17] Lord Saville was rightly scornful of the allegation made directly to Sir Edward Heath, when he gave evidence to the tribunal in Derry over eight days of oral testimony, that there had been a Cabinet agreement to shoot at protestors in Derry. The minutes of Cabinet meetings during the days before Bloody Sunday disclosed no conceivable warrant for alleging any conspiracy. At most there was only the flimsiest of suspicion gleaned from the documentation; it was at least inelegant to watch leading counsel for the families of the victims put the allegation forthrightly to Sir Edward, prefaced by the supposedly disarming statement that 'he [counsel] did not wish to be offensive, but …' to which Sir Edward replied with unerring perpendicularity: 'I *am* offended, and it isn't true'. Far from engaging in direct action against the notorious hooligans in Derry, Sir Edward Heath and his Cabinet colleagues had displayed, if anything, much too little active concern from Whitehall, with the hands-off policy towards the Stormont administration over the 50 years since the partition of Ireland.

---

[17] Mr Douglas Murray in his indispensable guide to what happened on Bloody Sunday—*Bloody Sunday: Truth, Lies and the Saville Inquiry* (Biteback, 2012)—pointed to the failure of the Inquiry to criticise General Ford for deploying the paratroopers in addition to adequate resident British regiments to police the march as surely a grave misjudgement.

Professor Paul Bew wrote in 2012, in a review of Douglas Murray's book on the Inquiry,

> Insofar as Heath had any sympathies on the Irish Question, they were pro-Catholic. He responded warmly to Garret FitzGerald's complaints about the treatment of Catholics in Belfast City government but would never have thought to ask about the treatment of Protestants in the same sphere in Dublin. He visited the Province before the Troubles began, to stay with Robin Chichester-Clark, the Ulster Unionist MP for Londonderry, but this does not seem to have influenced him in a pro-Unionist direction. He was proud of his decision to abolish Stormont in [March] 1972 and to force Ulster Unionist Prime Minister Brian Faulkner into accepting a very green-tinted power-sharing deal with an Irish dimension in 1974.[18]

But the examination of the 'conspiracy theory' was itself a costly, even marginal, exercise, ambitiously advocated.

Why did the Inquiry take so long and cost so much more than could reasonably have been expected when it was set up in 1998 (the estimates then were between 18 months and two years at a cost of £11 million)? The overriding reason for the vast expenditure in time and cost was the excessive dose (indeed an overdose) of legalism that was injected into, and overwhelmingly dominated the whole Inquiry which pursued the undoubted virtue of thoroughness, if appropriate. It failed instinctively to appreciate that it functioned, not as a court of law, but as an outreach of public administration. Therein lay the fundamental flaw. Thoroughness did not dictate proving every detail of a tragic event. It had to be treated as relative to the essential task of a public inquiry.

Lord Saville described the nature of his task in giving oral evidence to the Northern Ireland Affairs Committee of the House of Commons on 13 October 2010.[19] He said, in answer to the question about the time taken to report (12½ years):

> I did not comprehend it, because I had no idea how long it would last. We tried not to waste any time, but you have to remember that the Bloody Sunday inquiry was not, in fact, an inquiry *into one incident because we had to look at each individual shooting,* [italics supplied] because to do otherwise would be, apart from anything else, *grossly unfair to the soldiers concerned.* [italics supplied] You cannot paint them all black with one brush without giving each of them an opportunity to put his side of the story and, of course, that would take a very, very long time.

But the legal (criminal and civil) responsibility of the individual paratroopers was outside Lord Saville's duty; collective blameworthiness would have more than sufficed. In brief, the paratroopers' collective action of firing on the victims was the essential way forward.

The final cost of the Inquiry, not unnaturally, became the subject of acute political and public concern. When the House of Commons considered the Inquiry's

---

[18] *Literary Review*, February 2012, 21.
[19] HC 499-i published on 6 October 2011, at Ev 3.

report on 3 November 2010[20] the Conservative MP for South Staffordshire, Mr Gavin Williamson, drew attention to the desirability of budgetary control, and its absence from any consideration by Lord Saville. The estimate in 1998, on the basis of an 18 month to 2 year inquiry, of £11 million, he said, was 'either woefully optimistic or incredibly misleading'. He added:

> Lord Saville did everything he could to get at the truth and to ensure that he prepared a thorough and proper report, but he was in charge of the inquiry and he must therefore accept responsibility for its management and for the fact that, under his guidance, it went from £11 million and two years to not 10 times but almost 20 times that amount. As a member of the Northern Ireland Committee, I was struck by almost a disconnect when we interviewed Lord Saville: he had to manage the inquiry, yet he seemed to feel no responsibility for protecting the public purse as well as getting at the truth. I think that he would almost have gone so far as to say that the two were incompatible. I do not believe that that is the case. I have the perhaps slightly old-fashioned view that any public servant has a responsibility for public money. Lord Saville unfortunately disregarded that somewhat as he went through the many years before reaching the inquiry's conclusion.[21]
> [To which Lord Saville had earlier said:[22] 'I am a judge, not a politician'.]

The criticism of the cost and delay of the Inquiry was not confined to political statements and public opinion. It included the views of many people, including legal *cognoscenti*. In the *Belfast Telegraph* on 24 May 2012 Lord Woolf, a former Lord Chief Justice of England and Wales, was reported as being critical of Lord Saville. He is reported as believing that Lord Saville felt it was vital that everyone (including a company of paratroopers) had their say—not a matter of prime concern. According to the report, Lord Woolf stated:

> He was meticulous in that and very praiseworthy, but proportionality is very important and I just do not myself accept that any inquiry that took as long and involved the expense of the Saville Inquiry has not got things wrong ... I'm sorry to seem critical of an individual I admire, but that was what happened. How do you absorb all the information you have heard and record it even if you read and re-read it? It took a huge amount of time to do the report, everybody got a mention in the report who did anything, but the report is one which I doubt there is anybody in this country who has mastered the whole of the contents. It is beyond the capacity of a mortal individual ... They regarded themselves as having the ability to disregard expense.

## Legal Limitation on the Power of a Public Inquiry

Proceedings before a public inquiry do not fall within the scope of Articles 2 or 6 of the European Convention on Human Rights (except where Article 2 requires

---

[20] HL Deb 19 October 2010, vol 517, cols 951–1012.
[21] At col 1000.
[22] HC 499-I published on 6 October 2011, Ev 7 Q 22.

a coroner's hearing)[23]: a public inquiry does not constitute legal proceedings (whether civil or criminal) against any person.[24] Less still does it constitute a multiplicity of legal proceedings against each and every one of the witnesses subpoenaed to appear before it. If such were the case it would be impossible to conduct any inquiry. In that event, it would be necessary for each witness to cross-examine not only the witnesses who gave evidence before he did, but also that he should have the opportunity of cross-examining those who gave evidence *after* he had been heard. Even without that elaborate process of the legal system, the method of preparing written statements and oral testimony, tested sequentially, is arduous enough for any public inquiry. It bears its own burden of high costs. Furthermore, while the report of the tribunal may in its findings of fact contain criticism of the conduct of any person or persons who gave evidence before it, such findings are not determinative of their rights. The report is not even a stage in a process by which such rights are determined. No thought was devoted to the fierce criticism of Salmon Letters (which are dealt with earlier in this book).

The conclusions of the tribunal will not be evidence, either conclusive or *prima facie*, of the facts found by the tribunal. Moreover, the sponsoring minister may properly reject any findings and decline to act on any criticism against any individuals.[25] The public inquiry is an outreach of public administration, and is not within the legal system. Like any other ministerial or public authority, it is amenable to judicial review.[26] That was the clear law relating to public inquiries pre-2005, and is now declared statutorily in section 2(1) of the Inquiries Act 2005. The section has the heading 'No determination of liability' and provides, 'An inquiry panel is not to rule on, and has no power to determine, any person's civil or criminal liability'.

Sub-section (2) of section 2 qualifies the inquiry's limitation in the following way, 'But an inquiry panel is not to be inhibited in the discharge of its functions by any likelihood of liability being inferred from facts that it determines or recommendations that it makes'.

Assuming those provisions accurately declared the common law before 2005, what were the consequences for the Saville Inquiry in 1998? Why did it not look

---

[23] See Chapter 4 on the Jurisprudence of Public Inquiries.

[24] Elsewhere in this book I cite high judicial authority that the public inquiry system is 'sterile of legal effect' (see Brennan J in *Victoria v Australian Building Construction and Building Labourers' Federation* (1982) 152 CLR 25).

[25] The best exposition of the English common law relating to public inquiries is to be found in the judgment of Murphy J in *Lawlor v Flood* [1999] 3 IR 107 at 42–43, and see also Hardiman J in *O'Callaghan v Mahon* [2006] IR 32 at 74. Also the Supreme Court of Canada in a case reported at (1997) 3 SCR 440.

[26] Thrice during the hearings the Inquiry's decision on procedural matters concerning respectively the soldier-witnesses' right to anonymity (twice) and the appropriate venue for the taking of their evidence orally, was tested by way of judicial review. In each instance the ruling of the Inquiry was reversed by the Administrative Court (whose ruling was then upheld by the Court of Appeal) on the grounds of procedural fairness. One was unreported, the others are: *R v Lord Saville of Newdigate, ex p A* [2000] 1 WLR 1855 and *R (A and others) v Lord Saville of Newdigate and others* [2002] 1 WLR 1249.

for short cuts (such as collective responsibility) which could not disturb a finding of the cause of death? There was a double bind. First of all, there was the implied prohibition on the inquiry ruling on any person's civil or criminal liability; and secondly, the inquiry had no power to determine any person's civil or criminal liability (there may not be any difference between the two functions, but the statute seems to draw some distinction). These are matters exclusively for courts of law. Section 2(2) provides that liability may be inferred from the facts determined by the Inquiry and from the recommendations that it may make. There is thus a dividing line in the two parts of section 2 between prohibited and permitted findings by the inquiry. The result is that the inquiry may make findings of fact from which civil or criminal liability may be inferred, but it may not make rulings on civil or criminal liability. The inquiry might conclude that it would be preferable not to blur the distinction, and decide not to allow any inferences of liability to be drawn from its findings. It can do so only by itself declining to draw any inference or indicating that no inferences should be drawn by the reader of its report.

By their very nature, events under scrutiny often arouse strong feelings, particularly following politically sensitive, high-profile, controversial events where the sponsoring minister (in this case the Secretary of State for Northern Ireland) might, reflecting the views of the victims' families and other members of the public, expect the inquiry to determine who is to blame for what has occurred (Bloody Sunday must rate as a prime example). Given the prohibition, and the permitted findings, the inquiry may of course make a declaration of wrongful acts or omissions and of intentional or negligent acts or omissions. But the tribunal must keep in the forefront of its deliberations the concept that the main aim of public inquiries is to seek to restore public confidence in systems or services which underpin the day's military operation by way of safeguards, by investigating the facts and making recommendations that serve to prevent recurrence of the event. The aim is not to establish liability or to punish anyone. Understandably, there is often a public urge to identify blameworthy persons for what happened—particularly if death has resulted from individual action. But that urge should not be instantly responded to by the tribunal, a process of fact-finding and conclusions in its findings, although to reject such a response must not hamper the inquiry in its investigations from a determination of any fact. Blameworthiness is a slippery tool, not lightly to be applied. Findings that point to blameworthiness are one thing; it is altogether another matter to criticise behaviour that indicates legal liability.

If the parameter of the determinative powers of the Saville Inquiry had been fully appreciated, there was at least an implied indication that the legal limitations played no part in the Inquiry's approach to the terms of reference. Throughout the hearings it was repeatedly stated by the Inquiry that it was not engaged in conducting a trial by the three judicial panellists. But the soldier-witnesses who had fired the fatal shots perceived themselves, not unreasonably, as defendants in the dock at the Old Bailey. Onlookers would have concluded that the paratroopers were the Inquiry's prime targets for blameworthiness. They were, if not palpably, on trial. One should add that as a result of the report in June 2010, the authorities have undertaken a criminal investigation. In November 2015, one paratrooper (labelled anonymously as L) was arrested and charged. Seven other paratroopers have begun proceedings for judicial review, to prevent any interrogation by the Northern Ireland Police Service about their part in Bloody Sunday. The threat of criminal proceedings seems never-ending.

## Proof of Blameworthiness

At the eleventh hour of the hearings before the Inquiry (on 7 and 8 June 2004, days 428 and 429) the Saville Tribunal entertained argument from counsel for the interested parties represented before it on the approach that should be taken by the tribunal in weighing the evidence and coming to factual conclusions. The forensic event was prompted by submissions from the military personnel that the tribunal, in criticising or blaming anyone for the deaths of unarmed civilians, should apply the appropriate evidential tests of civil and criminal proceedings. Why the issue of the requisite standard of proof was not determined at the outset of the Inquiry's task, back in 1998, seems odd, since it had been widely assumed throughout the Inquiry that 'the issues which [it] is required to rule upon necessarily include issues of criminal responsibility'.[27]

The Tribunal's counsel, Mr Christopher (now Lord Justice) Clarke, QC, at the June 2004 hearing, postulated that the formula which he submitted ought to be applied was as follows:

It [the Tribunal] is at liberty to and should reach such conclusions as it feels able to reach, provided that it identifies with an appropriate degree of precision what is its conclusion and the degree of confidence with which it reaches it.

This formula neatly separates out the process to be adopted by a public inquiry under the Tribunals of Inquiry (Evidence) Act 1921 (or indeed any public inquiry) from the process of a court of trial in civil or criminal proceedings, where rules relating to the burden and standard of proof are well understood and applied. This formula is reinforced by the classic statement of Lord Diplock in the Privy Council case of *Mahon v Air New Zealand* in 1983[28] where he said:

The technical rules of evidence applicable to civil or criminal litigation form no part of the rules of natural justice (or fairness). What is required ... is that the decision to make the finding must be based on *some* material that tends logically to show the existence of facts consistent with the finding and that the reasoning supportive of the finding, if it be disclosed, is not logically self-contradictory.[29]

---

[27] These were the words which Mr David Lloyd-Jones, QC (now Lord Justice Lloyd-Jones) uttered on the occasion of an interlocutory hearing on 8 April 2004 (see Day 319: 88.24–89.6).
[28] *Mahon v Air New Zealand* [1984] AC 808.
[29] At 821A.

If many tribunals of inquiry (1921 Act tribunals and other statutory and non-statutory public inquiries) have adopted the standards of proof in criminal or civil proceedings,[30] they were wrong to do so. But why were the paratroopers not alerted to that when they came to the witness box?

The Inquiry emphatically rejected the notion that it was its function to determine rights and obligations of any nature. Its task was to investigate the events of Bloody Sunday, to do its best to discover what happened on that day and to report the results of its investigation. Its ruling of 11 October 2004 deserves recitation in part:

> 20. We now turn to the suggestion that it would be unfair to the individual to make findings implying criminal or other serious wrongdoing without applying the suggested standards of proof.

> 21. What was said on this was that the consequences of a finding implying wrongdoing on Bloody Sunday would be extremely serious for the individuals concerned, particularly so having regard to the standing of the Inquiry, the fact that it is charged to report to Parliament, the widespread publicity which its findings will undoubtedly rightly attract and the possibility that an individual may, as a result of the outcome be exposed to the risk of prosecution …

> 23. In our view, provided the Tribunal makes clear the degree of confidence or certainty with which it reaches any conclusion as to facts and matters that may imply or suggest criminality or serious misconduct of any individual, provided that there is evidence and reasoning that logically supports the conclusion to the degree of confidence or certainty expressed, and provided of course that those concerned have been given a proper opportunity to deal with allegations made against them, we see in the context of this Inquiry no unfairness to anyone nor any good reason to limit our findings in the manner suggested. Thus, to take an example, we cannot accept that we are precluded in our report from analysing and weighing the evidence and giving our reasons for concluding *that in the case of a particular shooting, we are confident that it was deliberate, that there was no objective justification for it,*[31] and though we are not certain, that it seems to us more likely than not that there was no subjective justification either. Of course we would have in mind the seriousness of the matter on which we were expressing a view, but that is not because of some rule that we should apply, but rather as a matter of common sense and justice.

The Inquiry duly rejected the submission in 2004 that, in reaching conclusions on matters implying criminality or serious misconduct, it should do so only on the basis that it was 'sure beyond a reasonable doubt'.

Two points emerge. Once the Inquiry had embarked upon an exercise that envisaged criticism of an individual that implied criminality or serious misconduct, there was the danger that the conclusions reached might be couched in language

---

[30] For example, in the Stephen Lawrence Inquiry in 1999 (Sir William Macpherson) and the North Wales Child Abuse Inquiry in 2000 (Sir Ronald Waterhouse) there were indications of the tribunals applying the criminal standard of proof.

[31] Italics supplied.

that the untutored public might perceive as showing some criminal or civil culpability to have been found. All too easily the dividing line between prohibition and permissibility would be breached. The collective culpability of those paratroopers who fired the fatal shots surely would suffice to assuage the wounded feelings of the secondary (family) victims as well as, one would hope, the populace of the Province and the rest of the world. Rather more relevant, blame (if any) might be more appropriately attributable to those in command of the paratroopers. Whatever the responsibility might be for those who fired the fatal shots, the military operation, devised by the General Officer Commanding (NI) and his advisers, who devised the day's operation and its implementation, might deserve rather closer scrutiny.

The second point relates to the timing of considerations by the Inquiry of potential criminality or serious misconduct. Had that ruling of October 2004 on the standard of proof in the context of findings of individual blame been articulated six years earlier, and had the issue been considered in the context of an interpretation of the Inquiry's terms of reference, the proper scope of the Inquiry could have been publicly aired and tested. The Inquiry rightly stated that the question was whether the shooting of civilians by soldiers was or was not justified. But to answer that question, was it necessary, even under the guise of thoroughness, to target the individual soldiers and inflict on them individually the most serious criticism—as distinct from a collective responsibility—having regard to the ambit of an inquiry into an event 30 years ago, with the prospect of a lengthy investigation and commensurately high cost? That question was never explicitly asked, and never formally answered. It should have been, as an essential aspect of fairness to the public generally, as well as for a huge saving of costs. An assumption from the outset of avoiding any question of criminal liability would have evoked some retreat from blameworthiness.

# 6

## The Lapse of Time:
## Assessment of Evidence[1]

### Evidence, Three Decades On: The Reliability
### of Witnesses

The Inquiry's chosen route of investigation, to find which paratrooper fired a shot from his rifle that killed the individual victim, unarmed and fleeing from gunfire, depended extensively on detailed reliable and credible evidence from those who witnessed the fatal shot(s), and corresponding evidence from the relevant paratrooper(s), including each soldier's state of mind in firing the shot. In order to substantiate from that massive amount of evidence individual criminality or serious misconduct on the part of any single paratrooper, the Inquiry set itself the formidable (if not unattainable) task of analysing and weighing all the evidence and giving its reasons for concluding that each shot fired was—to use the Inquiry's *ipsissima verba*—'deliberate and that there was no objective justification for it' ... and that 'there was no subjective justification for it'. That approach added immensely to the complications of individual responsibility. To reach such a finding rested quintessentially on the witness-testimony of happenings that took place 30 years ago. Compared with the evidential material placed before Lord Widgery, within a few weeks of the event, Lord Saville was faced afresh (since he had decided to start with a clean slate) with the daunting prospect of evaluating eye-witness testimony, not a few months, or even only a few years after the event, but three decades, not from just a few witnesses but from a plethora of them. Should the lapse of time also have been taken into account in the Inquiry's chosen route of investigation? Or would it have been enough to identify the validity or otherwise of the system and services that put into operation and sustained the military action to police the march, on the more rational footing of a collective responsibility for the fatal shootings?

Assessing the reliability of and evaluating eye-witness testimony is, at the best of times, never easy. The problem of memorising the event, together with the time

---

[1] The author has relied heavily on the academic literature on forensic psychology for much of this chapter, on the memory of witness testimony.

and space between the event and the recounting of it in the courtroom is always complex. But distancing the witness's experience from the retelling of it, assuming an ability to remember, does not produce instinctively an adverse result, although the lapse of time from the event to its retelling must arouse doubts about the reliability of the evidence. Putting aside the recovery of fresh material, which may positively inform the tribunal as well as affect a witness's evidence, and hence may approximate more nearly to the truth, was it, in practice, a fruitless exercise to expect a witness to state publicly what he or she saw and heard three decades ago? Broadly speaking, the psychology of testimony of public events does not provide a simple answer. A public inquiry into a national disaster may gain in public acceptance of its findings by the recency of the event and proximity of the report. Speed of determination is a highly desirable aim. But an unhurried examination, in amplitude, of the evidential material, with all the imperfections of delayed examination and reliance on long-term memory possesses the virtue of reflective examination and studied thought. If those thoughts were entertained by the Inquiry, the inherent problems of long-delayed testimony should have instantly caused the Inquiry to question the full implications of 'thoroughness' in the investigation. 'Thoroughness' might have to be tempered by the circumstances of limitation in time.

## A Second Bite

But Bloody Sunday was, at least in one sense, unique. The tribunal did not have to start from square one, even if it treated the material before Lord Widgery, adduced in February and March 1972, as *tabula rasa*. Most public inquiries have to find the facts for the first time (the fire at King's Cross station is a classic example) and start afresh on fact-gathering.

Rarely can such an event as Bloody Sunday have been so amply documented at the time and saturated by media coverage. Journalists had been forewarned of a significant demonstration of opposition to internment and other governmental acts arousing the ire of civil libertarians, as well as alerting the authorities policing the march. Together with TV and radio crews, broadcasters and journalists flocked to Derry in large numbers to report on the march. In the result, the later inquiry was able, uniquely, to draw on a vast amount of photographic material, intercepted messages from army radio links, newspaper reportage and the subsequent product of investigative journalism, particularly by the assiduous team at the *Sunday Times*. Media personnel were available to provide additional testimony to their recorded material. Armed with the mass of documentation, the Saville tribunal nevertheless embarked upon an exercise of oral testimony occupying oceans of time at inordinate cost, far beyond the established evidence. Given the aim of thoroughness in pursuit of aspirational truth, it is questionable whether it was necessary to do anything other than assess the evidence from contemporary written statements, judged alongside any previous documentary material and the unearthing of other documentary material. It is, no doubt, the English devotion to the orality of the forensic process that tends to value testimony by live witnesses in front of the tribunal, over and above the witness's written statement, whether professionally prepared or inexpertly recorded. Orality can, however, be too readily overvalued—a fact which should have led the Inquiry to adopt (or at least give due consideration to) a less expensive process.

It is widely recognised that, all other things about interesting events being equal (which they never are), memory plays tricks with human accounts of past events. Distortion of the memory is an ever-present factor. So too, the facility of conflation, not to say confabulation, is a potential source of distraction from the truth. It is a general proposition that events can be erased from memory; they are too uncomfortable to remain in the consciousness and are effectively suppressed. Likewise, they can all too readily be embellished by fertile imagination. But memory can survive in a reliable form. All these factors have to be reckoned with in any proper assessment of evidence. There are, however, some basic principles that should instinctively inform any tribunal seeking to find the facts. Retrospect is an uncertain activity. To apply it calls for careful attention to the judgment of a witness's credibility and reliability.

Human beings everywhere are equipped with eyes and ears which function in very much the same way to capture what is seen and heard. Yet accounts of an accident or an incident involving two or more people are sometimes given in contradictory ways by different observers, whether by journalists in newspapers or even in the courtroom. Such disparate, if not distorted, reports indicate merely that we do not see with our eyes alone or hear with ears alone. We see and hear with our whole person; and under certain conditions our eyes and ears become instruments which serve our desires, partisanship and biases. We are all the creatures of precondition and prejudice. Bias is altogether another dimension. As Jerome Frank, in his *Courts on Trial*, neatly observed, if we confuse these attributes with bias, then nobody has ever had or ever will have a fair trial!

Even if the civilian witnesses in the Saville Inquiry were not actively engaged in adversarial litigation, they brought with them strong emotional reactions to the violent (not to say, the political) aspects of Bloody Sunday. Families and friends of those who survived to tell their tales might understandably have coloured their testimony with the personal outrage of what happened to those who died. Others who were unhurt physically also brought to their testimony attitudes that infected their evidence. Observers on the march, who exhibited a certain detachment from, and objectivity to the events they described, could be more readily relied upon. The Inquiry needed no reminding of the inherent socio-political bias of most of those on the march, and hence deeply affected by Bloody Sunday. The factor peculiar to unexpected disasters, such as a shooting by armed forces on a civilian population, deserves special mention. Witnesses to a killing or wounding may be direct and compelling. But in a situation where civilians are fleeing from the scene of shooting, the individual would focus on the danger he or she feared, rather than on the cause of the fear. His or her testimony would relate to the perceived danger rather than a detailed account of the incident. By targeting an exclusive factor, the likelihood is that any detailed account by the witness will be lost.

Apart from such special aspects of recalling the events of 30 January 1972, there are some general principles that relate to the giving of eye-witness evidence. When a witness testifies in court or tribunal, what is he or she doing? A witness is not a photographic plate or a gramophone record. He or she is reporting a present memory of something observed in the past, something seen or heard in the fullest sense of sight and sound. A credible witness is a person willing to give what he or she believes to be accurate, reliable and complete information. This indicates that the credibility of a witness consists of two basic components. The first component relates to the ability of the person to give reliable evidence at one given point of time—a snapshot of the day's events. The second, separate component is the willingness of the witness to tell the truth. This relates to the motivational aspects of credibility; is the witness motivated to tell the truth? One can assume that all civilian witnesses to the tragedy on Bloody Sunday (perhaps, with some exceptions) were motivated to tell the truth. Courts are familiar enough with this phenomenon of self-deception or other deceptions (lying to others); tribunals, less anchored by legal rules, may, however be more or less wary of oral testimony.

It is the ability to account for information that is required, rather than to describe the actual event accurately. There are two groups of persons who are said to be peculiarly vulnerable to giving erroneous testimony, for one or both of two main reasons: (1) they are incapable of distinguishing fact from fantasy; this is referred to by psychologists as a breakdown in reality-monitoring; and (2) they tend to be unduly susceptible and acquiescent to questioning. This second reason need not detain us. This reason is relevant almost entirely to interrogation by, and confessions to, law enforcement agencies.

## The Memory Process

Memory, according to the clinical psychologists, is generally considered to be a constantly active and distortion-prone process. It can be directed theoretically within a tri-sequential framework. The first stage is *acquisition*. This involves the perception and encoding of the original event which is placed and interpreted in the context of the person's previous knowledge and experience. The information is instantaneous and forms the 'short-term' (working memory which retains information for a few seconds), persisting in the 'long-term'—more permanent—memory. The second stage is *retention*. This consists of the period of time between the observed event and evidential recollection. The third stage is *retrieval*. This involves the individual bringing back (recalling) the memory into current awareness. A number of factors affect the accuracy and completeness of memory at each of the three stages, each being involved in the Saville Inquiry. Broadly speaking, the various factors are influenced by the individual's abilities, past experiences, beliefs, personality and both mental and physical health. Additionally, environmental factors may be in play. Participation with others, known and unknown, on a civil liberties march which is banned by authority, cannot be discounted in any assessment of acquired memory. Indeed, a conscious act of joining a banned march may very probably have coloured or obscured the witness's memory at all three stages. As Bishop Daly tellingly observed in his evidence to the Inquiry, what else was left to the protesters at the denial by the Stormont Government of civil rights and liberties but to organise a peaceful march on the streets of Derry? Whether the ban on marches was indeed lawful in 1972 (as was the apparent reality), everyone acted on the assumption that the march was a breach of the law. I observe later in this book that it was the duty of the Inquiry to pronounce authoritatively what was the strict law in 1972. The published ban was not palpably enforceable legally. The presumption was that the official ban was interstitially enforceable. It must be assumed that the organisers of the march still thought that Article 11 of the European Convention on Human Rights imposed on the British government the obligation to observe this fundamental human right. Lord Saville did not mention this aspect of international human rights law.

## Acquisition of Memory

The stage of acquiring the perception and encoding of the original event (such as the multitudinous killings on that day) is affected by three interlocking factors: event and witness; stimuli and subject-matter; and situational or individual factors. Event factors are related to the nature and circumstances of the incident itself, whereas witness factors relate to the characteristics and limitation of the witnesses. The length of time people are able to observe a particular incident or event may affect the accuracy of their subsequent recall: the longer the observation, the more accurate the subsequent memory. And the more intensely people view—and review—an incident, the more likely they are to recall it. Where the observation is not focused at a particular time and space, but is spread over a period of time—eg a number of incidents taking place on and following the march—there is an opportunity for confusion (if not conflation) about the details of the incident(s), but the core of the observation is more likely to be firmly embedded in the memory and not readily distorted. Unusual, extraordinary and interesting details more readily attract attention than the insignificant and commonplace details.

There is some research finding that unexpected details or, even more so, surprising events, are better remembered than details that are consistent with expectations. The fact that rioting had become commonplace on the streets of Derry in the period before Bloody Sunday made it less likely that marchers would remember the rioting which took place at one point on the route of the march, at

Barrier 14. The usual inaccuracies occur with the reporting of time and space, they being the regular detailed segment of an event or incident in public. Overestimating the time that an event took is a common error. What is clear from all the research on the acquisitions of perception is the variation, often great, that occurs between people observing the same event, even if they are in close proximity to each other. Distances from the same incident may be viewed differently according to the positioning of the observer.

A number of studies have shown that the nature of the incident witnessed may significantly affect the subsequent accuracy of recall. The consistent finding of these studies is that events containing violent scenes are more poorly recalled than non-violent scenarios. The Inquiry could place greater reliance on those who described the peaceful nature of the march until the shootings began, than it could take on the early shooting during the march in William Street or, more so, the entry of the paratroopers at the end of the march, after 4.07pm on 30 January 1972, their entry onto the stage of the shootings. Where observers experienced high stress or unusual arousal in witnessing a violent event, there appeared to be a narrowing of the person's attention to the details of the incident.

Two researchers, SA Christianson and EF Loftus in a 1991 study, *Remembering emotional events: the fate of detailed information* in five experiments demonstrated that the relationship between emotional stress and memory is complicated, and statements that emotional events either lead to an impairment or enhancement in memory, depending on the circumstances, are an oversimplification. These two authors have drawn a clear distinction between memory for *central* as opposed to peripheral detail. Emotional stress tended to enhance memory associated with central detail; memory for peripheral detail is reduced. One interesting study in 1977 put forward the idea that major and surprising events—they gave as an example the assassination of a President—can result in exceptionally vivid, detailed and accurate memory traces of everything that was observed at the time. They labelled this type of memory as 'flashbulb' memory. Since people see and hear what they expect, desire or need to see and hear, and attitudes and beliefs, based on past experience, will inform their expectation, the effect on perception is crucial. Different types of expectation—cultural or stereotypes, past experiences, personal prejudices and preconceptions, and temporary expectations—can seriously distort people's judgments. Social expectations and political attitudes have been shown particularly to affect adversely perception and memory, the more so when the event observed is confusing, complex and within a short compass (around 15 minutes), as were the shootings on Bloody Sunday. More significantly, the killings by the company of paratroopers were recorded in sight and sound at the moment of their terrible consequences.

A number of experimental studies have shown that the elderly have poorer memory than younger subjects. The most reliable for eye-witness testimony are those who are physically active and inquisitive: the young. Since one of the Inquiry's witnesses was aged six at the time of Bloody Sunday, it is worth noting one study's findings that argued that childhood memories tend to be 'sparse and incoherent' and that relatively 'little is recalled of events occurring before the age of 7';[2] the authors explain this 'childhood amnesia' in terms of a young child not having developed the 'general knowledge schemas' necessary for interpreting and organising early autobiographical memories. The notion of schemas is that the processing of information is strongly influenced by pre-existing knowledge and experiences. The more one knows about a particular area of knowledge the easier it is to retain new information about it. Very young children lack that amount of knowledge. We are beginning to understand the nature of mental development, as witnessed by a recent spate of US Supreme Court cases on the sentencing of serious young offenders.[3]

## Retention of Memory

In the intervening period between acquisition and retrieval, memory generally becomes incomplete and less accurate, but the length of the intervening period may not be significant. Here the period was nearly 30 years. Memory loss may occur within a short time or it may survive over a long period of time, according to two types of factor: the 'retention interval' and 'the post-event interference', the latter of particular significance since the event of Bloody Sunday, sadly, has been awash with political propaganda, such that it impelled the setting up of a second inquiry.

### Retention Interval

Memory tends to deteriorate and become less accurate with time for a witnessed event. This appears to be due to ordinary forgetfulness, which is most rapid shortly after acquisition and then declines more slowly. Decline in memory and accuracy are, on the whole, related to the type of material observed. Face and voice identification are most prone to distortion, although some studies have indicated that accuracy is retained over extended intervals, over several months or years. Long delays are regarded, however, as highly undesirable. The distraction of memory by way of ardent political factors must have been a potent matter that calls for more reliance on the events that have been recorded, or subsequently investigated, even if that comes from investigative journalists.

---

[2] G Cohen, M W Eysenck and M E Levoi in *Memory: A Cognitive Approach* (Open University Press, 1986).
[3] See, for example, *Miller v Alabama* 132 S Ct 2455 (2012), where the US Supreme Court took a juvenile offender out of the adult criminal justice system—a hint, at least, of the abolition of capital punishment completely, where there is endemically a pronounced lack of mental development.

*Post-event Interference (Otherwise Known as Memory Contamination)*

A person is often exposed to fresh information, the more so when the event is witnessed by friends and neighbours, and has been covered by the media. While post-event information can not only enhance memories by the process of confirmation of what the person has seen, it can also change a witness's memory and even cause non-existent details to become incorporated into a previously acquired memory. The post-event information can be non-verbal, as well as verbal. One especial danger is that, after a while, witnesses may not be able to differentiate between their original perception of the event and the fresh information incorporated from external sources. Any intervening period, mingled with thoughts of wish-fulfilment, is apt to affect how events are remembered. Misleading information (mis- or disinformation) is more likely to distort memory when it is remembered by the witness after a long retention interval. Post-event information has its greatest impact when it is still fresh in a witness's mind. Witnesses are least likely to be misled about events which they can remember vividly. One factor relating to post-event information is the effect of discussion among witnesses before they give evidence (the paratroopers of the day, acting in consort together, will instinctively adhere to a single, often manufactured[4] story). This can potentially interfere with memory. In the case of the civilian witnesses before the Inquiry this cannot have been a potent factor other than in the context of the solidarity among the Catholic community in Derry. Contamination of the recall of other individual witnesses by prior group discussion, however, is a well-known psychological phenomenon, well understood in the criminal courts, and peculiarly relevant to the military solidarity of the soldier-witnesses. This applies specifically to the company of paratroopers, as distinct from the resident, regular soldiers policing the march. They, not unnaturally, exhibited group interests. If they felt under threat of inferred criminality or serious misconduct, the defence mechanism would be instinctive, and might seriously disfigure the value of their testimony. Yet the Saville Inquiry persisted in pursuing the exercise of extensive questioning and cross-questioning of the individual soldiers; there is little indication that the military personnel did not confer together in assimilating accounts of their actions, a factor well-noticed by Lord Saville—wisely so. Those who were participating professionally in the Saville Inquiry did not reject the notion of compliance in manufactured evidence. The Saville Inquiry testified that some witnesses palpably lied in their testimony, which is not surprising. This finding prompts the question, is not the fact of memory a vital element in determining the model of the investigation of a public inquiry? Would it not have been wiser to concentrate on the vast amount of contemporary literature, the later investigations of the journalists and the material that emerged in the years after January 1972? That alone would have supplied a huge amount

---

[4] One is forcibly reminded that the material advanced by the South Yorkshire Police in the wake of the Hillsborough disaster was a potent factor in delaying justice for 27 years.

of evidence; anything said between 1999 and 2004 can at best be regarded as supplementary. Above all, the testimony of the paratroopers in unison—much of it palpably lying—should have led to the rejection of their individual testimony.

## Retrieval

Much of the failure in memory results from the inability of witnesses to retrieve information rather than faulty acquisition or retention. A distinction is made between information potentially recoverable from the memory bank and that part of the bank which is actually accessible at any one moment. Only a small proportion of all memories are accessible on a given occasion. There are two methods for eliciting retrieval—recall, or recognition. A recall procedure means that a witness is presented with stimuli material, and then asked to report all that can be remembered. 'Free recall' means that there are no constraints placed on the witness with regard to recall. 'Cued recall' refers to witnesses being provided with specific cues to aid recall. This falls between free recall and recognition. The statements taken by Eversheds (the private firm of solicitors used by the Inquiry at considerable cost) must, by definition, be 'cued recall'. There is no knowing what 'cues' were used, or that the process of composing the written statements by the private firm of Eversheds was rigorously monitored by the Inquiry team. Presumably Lord Saville relied on the probity of that firm of solicitors.

Recognition means that witnesses are given one explicit cue which comprises the actual physical stimuli and involves genuinely effortless retrieval. Photographic material or documentary evidence may be presented years after, so as to prompt retrieval from the memory bank. This is a common technique of investigating bodies, including courts. Whether witnesses can retrieve information by recall or recognition depends on a range of factors. Events that are perceived and encoded during high levels of emotion tend to be less readily retrievable. But one study significantly demonstrated that, with time and perseverance into recall efforts, dramatic events may be successfully retrieved.

# Reality-monitoring

This psychological concept refers to the ability of the person to distinguish between two kinds of memory: (1) those resulting from external stimuli of experienced events through perceptional processes; and (2) those that are internally generated and relate to reasoning power, planning, imagining thought-processes. This inability to distinguish between the real as opposed to the imagined event can, and does, occur in everyday life. It is common for the recalling of an incident to be distorted by the fact of self-misconception of the incident itself. (The 'arrest operation' on 30 January 1972 was anything but a usual experience, even for paratroopers in the Province of Northern Ireland.)

Professor Arne Trankell, a Swedish psychologist, in his work *Reliability of Evidence*[5] recounts an episode revealing the mistakes that occur from the mechanism of logical completion. One day a lawyer was travelling in a taxi through one of Stockholm's busiest streets. Suddenly, the taxi was forced to make an emergency stop. At that moment the lawyer observed through the front window that the car in front had come to an abrupt halt. The lawyer saw the car's left back door had swung open, and noticed simultaneously that an old man either fell out of, or was thrown out through the open door and lay unconscious on the street. Some pedestrians hurried to assist the old man. The lawyer continued on his taxi journey. The next day, when he read an account of the incident in the newspapers (assuming the accuracy of the report) he discovered, to his great surprise, that his observations were mistaken. The car in front of the taxi had tried to avoid hitting the old man who had been walking across the street without looking where he was going. The unavoidable collision had resulted in the old man lying unconscious in the road and the open car door. These two impressions were translated into parts of a logical sequence which, although acceptable to the lawyer's mind, had little or nothing to do with reality. This story is a salutary reminder that those civilian witnesses who gave evidence to the Saville Inquiry may similarly have drawn logical conclusions about shootings by the paratroopers from a number of points of what was seen and heard on Bloody Sunday in a fast-moving shooting. The issue was complicated by the fact that the actions on Bloody Sunday, even if limited to what happened between 4 and 4.30pm, were multiple on the side of the military and multi-factored by the number of witnesses perceiving incidents from variable viewpoints—a whole series of snapshots. What a jumble to unravel. Yet the evidence of individual paratroopers was relied upon without, it seems to me, any recognition of its inherent unreliability. What the paratroopers did collectively sufficed for the purposes of assessing what happened on that tragic day.

Written statements made for the Widgery tribunal in 1972 had at least the prime quality of immediacy, or rather recency (with only a short time between the written statements and the oral testimony in which to reflect and be influenced by discussion). Even if it was right to start with a clean slate, the evidence of witnesses at the 1972 inquiry should have been preferred over later (post-1998) statements which provided the opportunity either, favourably, for memory-enhancement or lapses in memory or, unfavourably, for embroidered information. But the attitude of the individual at the time of making the statement may enhance, or detract from any reliability. The extensive literature about post-Bloody Sunday—almost all arguing volubly in favour of a fresh inquiry—must have been a factor influencing public opinion and individual attitudes to the event. The existence since

---

[5] A Trankell, *Reliability of Evidence: Methods for Analyzing and Assessing Witness Statements* (Beckman, 1972).

1972 of the established version of the events, as propounded inaccurately by Lord Widgery in his report, must have diminished in public acceptability, to the point where there was a presumption in 1998 of Lord Widgery's report being flawed. It has been dubbed as a 'whitewash', protractedly exposed to the shame of British justice, but it was forgivable, the inevitable consequence of assessing the reliability of witnesses, even at that time (February to March 1972). Saville thankfully erased a stain on that justice by starting afresh in 1998. But he was much too sweeping in his rejection of the material evidence that was proffered to Lord Widgery in 1972; that material was untainted by the lapse of time.

It is doubtful whether oral testimony based on the written statements composed erratically in the months after January 1998 significantly enhanced the degree of witness reliability. Indeed, there are grounds for thinking that orality serves more often than not to confuse the witness who has carefully composed his written evidence under professional guidance. An occasional illumination revealed by oral questioning in a formal setting has to be put alongside the undoubted value of contemporaneous written statements, even if orally untested. Where witnesses are uncertain about describing what has been seen or heard, it is better to leave the uncertainty undisturbed. Firming up an uncertain answer creates a serious doubt about the resultant 'certainty'.

The psychological experience of every civilian witness who marched or rioted on Bloody Sunday was a potent element in testimony reliability. Entrenched political and social attitudes could not be diminished, let alone altered by pleas of logic and rationality. Those civilian witnesses who were neither rioters nor marchers, but were non-participating observers (eg Knights of Malta first aid assistants) were intrinsically likely to give an objective account, particularly where photographic material supported their testimony. Where the witness's role was to observe and report on the event (eg journalists) there must be an inclination to rely heavily on such testimony.

The role and function of investigative journalism, however, is distinct from *reportage*. To the extent that investigative journalism may uncover material unavailable (or insufficiently available) to the Inquiry, such material may have been helpful in establishing what happened on the day in question, while comment and opinion on how and why the event occurred had a value only of a chronicled account with editorial interpretation. But investigative journalism, which was reliant upon recorded interviews with participants on the march (or other persons possessed of information about the circumstances leading up to or surrounding the march) would, one hopes, have been treated with special caution, particularly where the interviewee had not had the opportunity of checking and confirming (or otherwise) the contents of a journalist's notebook. There is great value in investigative journalism, but it too needs monitoring and assessing in the context of a free press.

The inestimable benefit derived from the vast amount of evidential material which the Inquiry had accumulated (both historically and contemporaneously) from the plethora of civilian witnesses (to say nothing of the huge collection of photographic and documentary material) should have led the Inquiry to adopt an overview of the march and the sequential shootings, rather than engage itself doggedly in detailed assessment of individual witnesses' accounts of a series of incidents, as if they were cameos or vignettes detached from the total picture. Systems and services must be the prime focus of any Inquiry, with less attention to individual culpability for what went wrong. Did the Inquiry really need to search for the truth whether 'in the case of a particular shooting' the shooting 'was deliberate [and] there was no objective justification for it'? The failure (developed later to consider factors leading up to the fatal day) to devote time to surveying the relevant systems for maintaining law and order in the Province produced in the report the lop-sidedness of this public inquiry.

All this evidence on the factor of memory argues forcibly for the decision-maker to mitigate or diminish the value of 'thoroughness'. A better approach would have been to assert effectiveness of the available material, as did the Council on Tribunals in its memorandum to the Lord Chancellor in 1996.

# Conclusion

It must be assumed that the political decision to re-open the 1972 inquiry was a factor in the process that led to the Belfast (Good Friday) Agreement of 1998. At that time, none of the parties to the conflict in Northern Ireland had agreed to a peace process that has ensued, unevenly, ever since. Until we have an account of the inner workings of government that led to the Good Friday Agreement, we will not know how significant the establishment of the Saville Inquiry was in persuading the Irish nationalists to reach that agreement. What we do know is that, apart from reviving, *in toto*, the terms of the Widgery inquiry, the method of proceeding was left entirely to Lord Saville, in the tradition of 1921 Act inquiries, of non-interference by the sponsor of the Inquiry with the way in which tribunals went about their investigations. Lord Saville and his colleagues were unaided in their interpretation of the general terms of reference. Therein, the fault may lie at the feet of the draftsmen, or, more particularly, with the lawyers who did not challenge the precise scope of the impending inquiry. The Inquiries Act 2005 has thankfully put an end to public inquiries other than at the insistence of a sponsoring minister of the Crown.

It may be that the political will in the twentieth century was to leave the Inquiry to encompass as many political outcomes as possible, for as many participants as possible within the scope of an inquiry which, as stated above, is not permitted to reach conclusions about criminal or civil liability. But whatever the outcome perceived by the sponsor of the terms of reference, the Inquiry was still left to determine its own interpretation of what was being asked of it. Did the political background to the Inquiry lead Lord Saville inexorably to adopt the expansive role (the *soi-disant* 'thoroughness'), and to want to listen to the huge amount of evidence that he did, or was an alternative, shorter route of investigation sensibly open to him?

By any objective standard (without resorting to hindsight, sometimes called 'retrospectiveness') the terms of reference of 29 January 1998 ought sensibly to have been interpreted to mean a public inquiry limited in practical application, according to the alternative approach suggested above. An early preliminary hearing in public, in the City Hall in Derry, should have provided the opportunity to the interested parties to consider the Inquiry's provisional decision, either to limit the scope of the Inquiry or steer it towards the extended purpose. As it transpired, the main topic of the preliminary hearing was related (I assert, fatally) to legal representation before the Inquiry. The scope of the Inquiry had been predetermined—on 21 July 1998, Christopher Clarke, counsel to the Inquiry, stated: 'As is well known, the function and the duty of an Inquiry appointed by Parliament is to make such investigations as are necessary in order, so far as it is possible to do so, to arrive at the truth'. Adherence to any decision about the Inquiry's *modus operandi* required a detailed reasoning for adopting or rejecting the expanded scope of the Inquiry. The decision on such an issue would have been judicially reviewable. Hence the courts could have been the final arbiter of the purpose of the Secretary of State for Northern Ireland's intention in ordering the public inquiry. The absence of any early decision by the Inquiry on the interpretation of its terms of reference deprived the Inquiry of a reasonable, well-directed and focused investigation into what went wrong, systematically and operationally, on Bloody Sunday, instead of a protracted investigation towards affixing culpability or serious misconduct on individual participants among the company of paratroopers, used exceptionally in an 'arrest operation'. To do the latter was to indulge in an unnecessary exercise beyond blame for the questionable military operation that ended in tragedy. The full application of the Six Cardinal Principles of the Salmon Report led to a seriously misdirected inquiry. A focus on the system and services that led to the tragic loss of life on Bloody Sunday was marginalised by the huge investigation into the liability of the individual paratroopers who fired the fatal shots.

That is not a criticism of the Saville Report itself. But what is to be faulted is the uncritical conduct of the Inquiry: it was insufficiently cognisant of the practice ever since the formulation of the Six Cardinal Principles of the Salmon Commission in 1966, and followed them religiously; the Saville Inquiry fully adopted the uniform practice of the legal profession to adopt the enhanced method of Salmon letters in the form of written statements, professionally prepared and processed, somewhat in the fashion of a criminal indictment or the particulars of claim in a civil suit.

# 7

## The Unexplained Circumstances

### Introduction

The function of the Six Cardinal Principles, although never adopted statutorily (but officially commended), was seriously questioned in the *Arms to Iraq* Inquiry in 1996. The falsity of the Salmon letters, exposed volubly and with justification by Sir Richard Scott and other chairmen, was impliedly rejected by Lord Saville. He should at least have indicated why he adhered to the established system; more still he should have queried the use of a procedure about the legal representation of witnesses, if only to have reinforced the desire to adopt a more limited mode of conducting a public inquiry. Additionally, the uniqueness of the accessibility of a mass of documentary material from the media which covered the march should have led to a more limited mode of the Bloody Sunday Inquiry.

There is nothing in the Saville report to suggest that the tribunal did not take full account of facts that might militate against the validity of the finding which entirely vindicated the marchers from any improper conduct in exercising their right to march in procession through the streets of Derry. Indeed, the report specifically exonerates the Northern Ireland Civil Rights Association from any blameworthiness in organising and managing the march, thus repudiating emphatically what Lord Widgery had concluded. That finding of exoneration of the marchers and the responsibility of the paratroopers is to be admired. But at what price?

There is also absolutely nothing to suggest that the Saville Inquiry neglected to take account of the effects of the credibility and reliability of the witnesses who recalled their memory of a tragic event. It must be accepted as reasonable to assert (as I do) that such issues relating to evidence of the events on Bloody Sunday were not overlooked, or insufficiently informed the judgments of that evidence; clearly they were considered in the massive investigation over such a length of time. Vindication of the marchers in exercising their civil liberties irrespective of the ban on marches would have been just as much the conclusion of a less expensive system than that which cost the public purse over £200 million, as well as misunderstanding the real purpose of a public inquiry: to consider the background to the policing of the march and the use of the 'arrest operation' effected by the paratroopers on the ending of the procession.

Other than the eliciting of written and oral evidence, the Inquiry adopted self-inflicted attitudes that indicated the procedure of the hearings—not adversarial, but inquisitorial, Salmon-style. As a coda, I hint that society could usefully evaluate the process of orality in the age of digitalisation (an ugly excretion of modern language).

# Legal Representation

At an early stage the tribunal expressed its provisional view, in a paper summarising matters to be discussed, that the interests of the victims' families would be met, not unreasonably, by representation from one leading counsel and two juniors. At its preliminary hearing on 20/21 July 1998—and in a finding of 24 July 1998—it changed its mind, as a result of a submission made by Mr Seamus Treacy QC (now Mr Justice Treacy) instructed by Belfast solicitors, Madden & Finucane. The change was to accept a team of *five* Queen's Counsel and *five* junior counsel. They were all granted reasonable costs from public funds for the duration of the Inquiry 'in the task of identifying and locating those who may be able to help the Inquiry'.

No question arose about the propriety of conferring legal representation on interested parties, as it should have. It was assumed—not without some justification—that fairness to the families of the victims who had been found blameworthy by the first public inquiry by Lord Widgery in 1972 required that 'justice should not only be done, but be seen to be done'. No thought was devoted to the status of witnesses (only the wounded among the victims and other observers of the march could be available to testify) in a public inquiry. As the Court of Appeal was to explain in *R (Main) v Minister for Legal Aid*,[1] the common law did not require that the claimant in a coroner's inquest into the deaths of his mother and sister following a railway accident in November 1994 should be publicly funded. Neither did Article 2 of the European Convention on Human Rights and Fundamental Freedoms import a duty on a public authority to provide public funds to avoid a breach of the Convention's right to life:[2]

> The European Court of Human Rights has established two general principles in relation to Article 2. First, the requirement that 'everyone's right to life shall be protected by law' imposes a primary duty on the State to put in place a legislative and administrative framework designed to provide effective deterrents against threats to the right to life. Secondly, where lives have been lost in circumstances potentially engaging the responsibility of the State, Article 2 entails a duty on the part of the State to ensure an adequate response, judicial or otherwise, so that the legislative and administrative framework set up to protect the right to life is properly implemented and any breaches are met

[1] *R (Main) v Minister for Legal Aid* [2007] EWCA Civ 1147.
[2] ibid, para 44.

by an appropriate penalty (see, for example, *Oneryildiz v Turkey* (2005) 41 EHRR 20 at paras 89 and 91, and the cases there cited.)

Lord Justice Carnwath (now Lord Carnwath, a Supreme Court Justice) sitting with Sir Igor Judge (later Lord Judge, Lord Chief Justice) and Lord Justice Toulson (until 2016 a Justice of the Supreme Court), held that guidance under section 23 of the Access to Justice Act 1999 indicated that legal aid funding for advocacy services to interested parties was normally excluded. That guidance adopted the general principle that an inquest held in public was inquisitorial and not an adversarial process; the coroner—*a fortiori*, the commissioner of a public inquiry—could reasonably be expected to carry out a proper investigation into the deaths of the deceased without the assistance of counsel for any victims' families. An inquest or public inquiry, including investigations into the wider aspects of safety issues, could not be assisted by lawyers acting on behalf of interested parties. The coroner had a discretion as to whether he might be assisted if the victim's family were legally represented. So too, the chairman of a public inquiry.

Assuming that the victims of the Bloody Sunday tragedy deserved to be exonerated from any blame for their deaths (in direct defiance of the finding to the contrary, thirty years earlier by Lord Widgery) why were ten counsel and instructing solicitors necessary, as opposed to one QC and two junior counsel and solicitors? It is hard to imagine why the tribunal was persuaded to abandon its provisional view. The tribunal's reasoning does not bear close scrutiny; it (the tribunal) would presumably obtain as much assistance from two advocates as from ten, unless help was needed to advance the eliciting of witnesses. As for counsel's instructing solicitors, the Inquiry stated that in particular, the legal representatives of the victims' families involved the work to be undertaken by the solicitors whose duty it was 'to be responsible for collecting, collating, analysing and presenting all relevant material'. This 'duty' would, of course, be in addition to the task of the Inquiry's team in presenting the evidential material for the tribunal.

Two courses of early action presented themselves; neither appeared to be considered. The tribunal could have looked to the sponsoring author—in this case the Secretary of State for Northern Ireland—for elucidation of the terms of reference. It is always possible for a minister to be asked what precisely he or she wants inquiring into; unlike a judge in a court of law, a commissioner of inquiry is always in post to do the bidding of the ministerial requirement as to the scope of the inquiry, but otherwise the minister must not intervene. The alternative was for the tribunal to pose the problem in a preliminary hearing for the interested parties to air their views about how the terms of reference should be interpreted. Any doubts about accommodating different views on that score could have been resolved by way of judicial review in the courts of law. But those options seem never to have been contemplated. The tribunal had predetermined its course of action, and that was that. Had the scope of the Inquiry not been pre-determined at the July preliminary hearing, and instead discussed with the legal representatives, the amount of such legal representation might have indicated a less ample assistance from their clients.

# The 'Arrest Operation': Its Origins

Causality for the fatal shooting of the 13 unarmed victims arose only indirectly from the civil rights march in procession in Derry on 30 January 1972: it was the firing of shots indiscriminately at fleeing marchers from the intruding company of paratroopers, in the space of 15 minutes of chaotic violence at the end of the procession. Until that moment the paratroopers had been assembled in reserve at the back of the line of regular battalions of the British Army policing the organised procession. The paratroopers were acting in accordance with the order of what was dubbed as an 'arrest ('scoop-up') operation' subsequent to the march. The 'arrest operation' was authorised and orchestrated by General Robert Ford[3] as an adjunct to the march, and designed to root out the 'hooligans' who had been in recent weeks engaged as troublemakers disrupting the commercial life of the city. Apart from a general plea of the policing authorities that the firing was preceded by a single shot, thought to have emanated from a hostile source in or around the city walls, none other than the assumed shot from a terrorist soldier was identified. The paratroopers were then ordered to 'scoop up' the relevant marchers. The subsequent shooting took place in the course of a quarter of an hour, at around 4pm on a sunny afternoon. The killing of the 13 was indisputably from the paratroopers; their presence was the design of the Commander of Land Forces, Northern Ireland, General Ford. They had been introduced to the Province only days before the event and were not employed other than for special duties to effect, if necessary, the 'arrest operation'.

The first original documented evidence of the plan to arrest 'the hooligans' or rioters with the use of 1 PARA, if and when rioting proved to be an outcrop of the public disorders, emerged only from the pen of the Brigade Major of 8 Brigade (Colonel Steele) overnight on 26/27 January. *Operation Forecast* appeared as a Brigade Order, dated 27 January 1972, and marked SECRET on 28 January 1972. It was *not* presented to the Joint Security Committee at its meeting of 27 January 1972, and no mention of an impending 'arrest operation' was noted. *Operation Forecast* was given a circulation beyond its immediate author and the Brigade Commander only as and when it was discussed at the Co-ordinating Conference held at Brigade HQ at 14.30 hours on 28 January, and even then the Brigade Order was limited to those at senior army level (all Commanding Officers) directly involved in the security operation for the day. Chief Superintendent Lagan (the chief police officer in Londonderry) attended the co-ordinating conference but did not speak (he had previously expressed the view that the civil rights march should be allowed to take place, despite the ban). Brigadier McLellan told him at the Saturday briefing

---

[3] General Sir Robert Ford died on 27 November 2015. His obituary in *The Times* recorded that he had not made any public statement as a result of the publication of the Saville Report on 20 June 2010.

session on 29 January 1972 that 1 PARA would be carrying out the arrest operation. While the Army's plans to deal with the impending march were generally known at that time to both the senior military and RUC officers, knowledge of the 'arrest operation' was restricted to a select few. There is no documentary evidence that politicians in Northern Ireland were aware of the 'arrest operation', although attendance at unscheduled and unrecorded meetings between the Prime Minister of Northern Ireland and his General Officer Commanding (NI) (abbreviated to GOC) might have revealed what was afoot. Evidence of this *ad hoc* security committee that included Brian Faulkner, Chief Constable Shillington and the GOC was given to the tribunal. No record of matters raised at the secret *ad hoc* security committee meetings was kept. Since the tribunal was without evidence from two actors in the scenario for security operations, the question whether, and to what extent, the GOC as Director of Operations was influenced politically had to go unanswered. Certainly, the governmental instrument of security policy and practice—namely, the Joint Security Committee (JSC)—was unaware of *Operation Forecast* or any hints of what it contained, other than the Army's plans for policing of the march on a prescribed route.

Nothing said at the JSC meeting of 13 January 1972 referred specifically to the impending NICRA march planned for 30 January 1972. During the discussion on the current security situation, General Tuzo indicated that, following a meeting with businessmen in Derry—presumably a reference to General Ford's visit to that city on 7 January 1972—'certain measures were in hand with a view to putting down the troublesome hooligan element there'. The GOC added, prophetically: 'it was a very difficult problem to solve within the law'. The Delphic reference to 'certain measures' may have been a reflection of the comment of an officer in the Northern Ireland administration, Mr Maurice Harris, that 'if an operation was being planned which required a degree of secrecy for its success the GOC might not have wanted to discuss details at a full meeting of the JSC'.

At the meeting of the JSC on 27 January 1972 the minutes recorded as follows:

> The Londonderry Marches[4] presented more serious difficulties and security action will be primarily an Army operation ... The basic plan here will be to block all routes into William Street and stop the march there. The operation might well develop into rioting and even a shooting war ... Prosecution for breaches of the ban on processions was disappointingly low.

The two members of the JSC who might conceivably have been aware of any arrest of hooligans on 27 January 1972 were the GOC and the Chief Constable. Sir Graham Shillington, in his written evidence to the Inquiry, had said that he did not believe that 'he was aware that the Parachute Regiment were going to be involved in the march'—an arrest operation is not a natural corollary to the policing of

---

[4] Presumably this referred to the two marches—the one from the Creggan and the other from Shantallow, the latter subsequently aborted.

a march—and that he did not remember actually discussing the arrest operation at the Director of Operations meeting on 26 January, and he personally had no active involvement in the practical details of the day.

Chief Superintendent Lagan, responsible for the police service in the county of Londonderry from 1969 until his retirement in 1973, made a written statement to the Saville Inquiry, but was too ill to give oral evidence. On the question of the march he asserted that 'Bloody Sunday was the first occasion that I had been at variance with the Army', but that 'at no time did General Ford consult me in relation to the march: I had not spoken individually to General Ford on any matter'.[5] At paragraph 65, Frank Lagan concluded that 'I was never told why 1 PARA were brought to Londonderry on Bloody Sunday or why they were used for the arrest operation'. On the propriety of the civil rights march itself, his advice jointly made with Brigadier Maclellan (with whom he consulted regularly about law and order), 'that the march ought to be allowed to proceed',[6] was rejected by the Chief Constable of the RUC.

Nothing was in fact communicated either to the RUC or the JSC that 1 PARA had already been deputed earlier in the week to go to Derry to fulfil its allotted task of 'scooping up' prospective rioters. Lieutenant 026, an officer in C Company of 1 PARA, told the tribunal that 1 PARA were 'not expected to carry out any static duties', implying that he and his colleagues knew that 1 PARA was engaged exclusively to carry out the arrest operation. Only the military, however, was privy to the plans for the arrest operation.

If General Tuzo was not revealing beyond military sources the 'certain measures' he was anticipating to deal with rioters, the Ministry of Defence and the Home Office in London could have known about the arrest operation from either the GOC or the UK representative at the JSC. It would not have obtained the information from Northern Ireland sources or the JSC itself. The information about the Army plans for policing the NICRA march might have been gleaned from the GOC in performance of his obligation to inform those in military authority 'up the chain of command as far as the Defence Council and ultimately to Her Majesty'. What precisely, if anything, did Whitehall know of the Army's plans for policing the march and the arrest operation on 30 January 1972?

The focal point of non-military Whitehall attention to Northern Irish affairs resided in the unit (DS10) within the Ministry of Defence headed by Mr A W Stephen, an Assistant Secretary in the Ministry. To the extent that anyone in the UK administration (politicians and civil servants) knew of the Army's plans, such knowledge would inevitably have filtered through to Mr Stephen, whose memorandum of 26 January 1972 for the two meetings the following day—the Northern Ireland Policy Group and the GEN 47—adumbrated, without

---

[5] para 52, JL 10.
[6] para 50.

elaboration, arrests of marchers and possibly rioters, once the march had run its course. His note stated:

> The GOC and UK Rep consider, and the Home Office and MoD are inclined to agree, that it would however be unwise to attempt to arrest any prominent political figures who happen to be in the van of the march, since this would be quite likely to precipitate really serious rioting. For such people, the only feasible course remains to take out summonses as soon as possible afterwards. It might be difficult then to arrest others among the marchers, while ignoring the leaders. However, there would be no objection to arresting anyone on the fringe of the march who was causing trouble; and it seems only too likely that, once the march is brought to a halt, there will then be at least some hooliganism. The GOC therefore has in mind to arrest a fair number of such hooligans and to arrange for a special court sitting on Monday morning, before which they can be brought. [The suggestion of a special court for 31 January 1972 seems never to have been followed up.]

It is clear that General Ford was contemplating some positive action to arrest correctly anticipated rioting hooligans in connection with, and probably at the end of, the NICRA march. The passage did not, however, allude to General Ford's plan for the 'arrest operation' as part of the day's operation, and it in no way descended to particulars, but the similarities were striking. There was no inkling that 1 PARA (by that time alerted for action) was being exclusively deployed to effect an arrest operation. The passage places in context the comment of the GOC on 24 January 1972 that NICRA were 'the active ally of the IRA'.

Mr Stephen's superior, Sir Arthur Hockaday (now deceased), had not thought that any arrest operation was contemplated. He stated that 'the military operation was there to deal with the civil rights march'. But might not someone at the GEN 47 meeting have reasonably asked for particulars? And would not any such query have instantly prompted the production of *Operation Forecast*, available that day or within 24 hours? But the question was apparently not asked, and the plan for the arrest operation was not uncovered by questioning eyes. Since the policing of the march was recognisably a matter for the military, and any arrests would be associated with the march, the matter rested there. Questions should have been, and were not, asked.

The conclusion must be that the arrest operation, as devised in *Operation Forecast*, was a well-guarded secret, knowledge of it being almost entirely confined to the inner circle of the military hierarchy in Northern Ireland and London. Politicians at Stormont might well have known through the *ad hoc* security committee. There was also the contribution of Commander Anderson during the Stormont debate on 3 February 1972. The question, to which the tribunal might have provided an answer, is whether the GOC fulfilled his duty under the Directives of 1969/1971 to communicate, not just to military colleagues but also to Ministers of the Crown, the fact of the planned arrest operation on Bloody Sunday.

NICRA's answer was that, whatever the level and degree of knowledge about the policing of the march, the specific ingredient of the 'arrest operation' was conceived and implemented in total disregard of the military obligation to collaborate and co-operate with the RUC. The evidence of Sir Graham Shillington established that. In the light of the close personal and official relationship of General Ford to the Prime Minister of Northern Ireland, it could reasonably have been inferred that the Stormont government did have knowledge of the projected 'arrest operation' by 1 PARA on Bloody Sunday. If so, the Stormont government would, in its political role, have given the 'arrest operation' at least tacit approval. If there was any appreciation by Stormont politicians of what was envisaged in *Operation Forecast*, the 'arrest operation' was a pointless exercise[7] that should never have been contemplated.

The question was posed, and answered, whether there was any blame to be attached to the author and architect of the 'arrest operation' which led to the tragic deaths of the 13 victims. The Inquiry acquitted General Ford of any impropriety in working to deal militarily with the disturbances caused by hooligans. The responsibility for the 'arrest operation' was General Ford's as the commanding officer of the armed forces. But was that responsibility only a result of a military power?

# Public Disorder in Northern Ireland in 1972

Following the civil disturbances in Northern Ireland in 1969, UK ministers were propelled into direct involvement in Northern Ireland matters—in particular, the whole question of internal security in the Province, for which the Stormont administration had up until then been constitutionally responsible. The relationship between the armed forces of the Crown and the police authority in Northern Ireland (then the Royal Ulster Constabulary) was altered. Hitherto it had been the case that it would have been 'the height of folly for the British Government to allow its [British] troops to be under the political control of another Government ... Ministers believed that it would be equally unacceptable for troops to be used ... if they were to maintain law and order for the existing Northern Ireland Government'. An agreement of 19 August 1969 changed the constitutional position. What precisely was the position when the British Army agreed to take on the powers of the RUC 'in aid of the civil power'? The crucial question was: what did that entail in terms of the manner in which the armed forces would function as a military force or, since they were exercising the powers of the enforcement of law and order by the police, how should they adopt the approach of police, rather than that of a military force? The constitutional position in Northern Ireland was amply stated in evidence to Lord Saville by Sir Arthur Hockaday (AUS(GS) at the Ministry of Defence, since then, deceased) who in evidence referred to a letter of

---

[7] This was the view of Professor JJ Lee, University of Cork, in his book, *Ireland: 1912–1985: Politics and Society* (Cambridge University Press, 1989) 440.

12 May 1971 to Mr David West who was the civil adviser to the General Officer Commanding (Northern Ireland). Under the heading of *Executive Responsibility* Sir Arthur wrote:

> The soldier acts under higher military authority up the chain of command as far as the Defence Council and ultimately Her Majesty. The Secretary of State is the Minister Responsible to Her Majesty for everything connected with the performance of their military duties by the armed forces of the Crown ... for everything connected with the performance of their military duties the soldier is responsible to Her Majesty and to Westminster ... *in going to the aid of the civil power [the armed forces] should liaise with the civil authorities as closely as possible* and give their views all due weight, particularly on such matters as and when the intervention has achieved its objective; *but the wishes of the Civil Authority can in no way bind the Commander on the spot to a particular course of action or relieve him of legal responsibility* (italics supplied).

The submission made to Lord Saville was that in carrying out the function of aiding the civil power, there was a duty on the GOC and his staff to take fully into account (but not be bound by) the views of the senior police officers whose duties were being performed by the Army. Lord Saville understood the submission in effect to be 'the Army treated policing of civil disturbances in Northern Ireland as a military conflict with an enemy, whereas the police were trained to use force only as a last resort...' and was planning an 'arrest operation' by additional troops in the shape of paratroopers, with their propensity to engage in direct combat. Paratroopers would be used only to mop up the hooligans at the end of the civil rights march, which had been policed by the Army. The lining of the march's route by army regiments resident in Northern Ireland was unexceptional, both by military and police standards. What was unusual and untoward in police terms was General Ford's deployment of paratroopers positioned to engage in an 'arrest operation' against potential rioters at the end of the march; they did not take any part in the 'policing' of the civil rights march.

Whatever the merits or demerits of the submission, the response of Lord Saville revealed his approach to the question. The report states:

> In our view this submission is so broadly stated that to consider it would have required a wide-ranging investigation into the conduct of soldiers and police in Northern Ireland in the period leading up to Bloody Sunday, a task that it was simply impracticable for us to undertake.

It would not have been impracticable to consider the place of the military in aid of the civil power over the two years since the armed forces had been deployed in the Province, so long as the balance of the Inquiry's task, to discover why the tragic event had occurred, had been maintained. The constitutional doctrine is still pertinent and applicable to inform future liability. Lord Saville should not have been distracted from considering the role of the paratroopers on 30 January 1972, which would not have involved an inordinate amount of inquiry time. The doctrine of 'aid to the civil power' only functioned after August 1969 and operated until January 1972—not a very long inquiry to engage in.

## Aiding the Civil Power

No mention was made in the report of any consideration of the lone decision in *Attorney-General for Northern Ireland's Reference (No 1 of 1975)*,[8] where the House of Lords touched upon the doctrine (described as the 'citizen-in-uniform') in relation to the troops in Northern Ireland after their imposition in 1969 as an aid to the civil power. Military support to the police in its role of keeping public order may be temporary, such as in response to a severe riot, or a longer-term operation in cases of continuing, sporadic unrest, such as was the experience in Northern Ireland. The distinctions between military intervention was recognised by Lord Diplock, who said:[9]

> There is little authority in English law concerning the rights and duties of a member of the armed forces of the Crown when acting in aid of the civil power; and what little authority there is relates almost entirely to the duties of soldiers when troops are called upon to assist in controlling a riotous assembly. Where used for such temporary purposes it may not be inaccurate to describe the legal rights and duties of a soldier as being no more than those of an ordinary citizen in uniform. But such a description is in my view misleading in the circumstances in which the army is currently employed in aid of the civil power in Northern Ireland. In some parts of the province there has existed for some years now a state of armed and clandestinely organised insurrection against the lawful government of Her Majesty by persons seeking to gain political ends by violent means—that is, by committing murder and other crimes of violence against persons and property. Due to the efforts of the army and police to suppress it the insurrection has been sporadic in its manifestations but, as events have repeatedly shown, if vigilance is relaxed the violence erupts again.

If indeed there is scant authority to indicate the role and function of the deployment of armed forces as the sole police force to deal with civil disobedience, an authoritative finding of the system—not just the emergency in Londonderry in 1971/2—was called for to determine the blameworthiness alleged against General Ford, or at least the failure to canvass the use of temporary or timeless purposes. Lord Saville's claim was that 'it was simply impracticable for us to undertake' the task. In an informative article in *Public Law*,[10] Mr Stephen Spencer noted that the task of security forces in Northern Ireland was 'dangerous and difficult'. Nevertheless the innocent citizen (which the unarmed marchers were) could be in danger. He adds: 'Civilians have no protection but the judiciary. There is a need to establish clearly recognisable limits to the actions of the security forces'. Lord Saville was in effect being asked to make a start, which he rejected. Even now it is not too

---

[8] *Attorney-General for Northern Ireland's Reference (No 1 of 1975)* [1977] AC 105.
[9] At p 136.
[10] *Public Law* (2000).

late for the Parliamentary Committee on Northern Ireland to ask Lord Saville for further elucidation of the 'arrest operation' on 30 January 1972.

The Saville report's response also misunderstood what was being suggested—that is, a limitation on the GOC's power. Practicalities did not deter the Inquiry from considering, at length, an issue of the relationship of British Ministers to law and order in Northern Ireland, and comprehensively dismissing the allegation of ministerial conspiracies. No doubt the scope of the Inquiry was always a consideration, but if the Army was constitutionally to cope with the problems of maintaining security in the Province, and to hand back those powers as and when the disturbances were over, there is something to be said for the Army adopting the civilian approach to protecting the populace. Martial law had not been declared in Northern Ireland.[11] That situation is effective only in a state of war, armed rebellion or insurrection, which is in stark contrast to the military acting 'in aid of the civil power'.

At paragraph 2.3 of the Report, Lord Saville notes that on 14 August 1969 the authorities brought into Londonderry units of the British Army as an aid to the civil power, 'in other words, to establish law and order'. And he added that the 'British Army was in the city in this role on Bloody Sunday'. Lord Saville did not expound the elements of military aid to the police service, although in accepting the concept of supplanted power he points out that 'the problems facing the security forces were not just civil disobedience, but widespread civil disorder often accompanied by lethal paramilitary activity' (paragraph 193.47). Just so. Did not the concept of 'aid to the civil power' encompass a consideration of the precise scope of a soldier performing a policeman's function? And if so, the suggestion that General Ford never envisaged the use of armed paratroopers in an 'arrest operation' called for an examination of the concept—an exercise that did not require a study of the decision in 1969, but only a detailed analysis of the events in January 1972 prior to the civil rights march of the 30th of that month. That would at least have involved a limited part of the day's tragic event lasting no more than fifteen minutes. As Lord Saville notes (at 4.12) 'General Ford was responsible for deciding that in the likely event of rioting, Brigade [under Brigadier MacLellan] should employ 1 PARA as an arrest force on 30th January 1972', acknowledging that General Ford neither knew nor had reason to know at any stage that his decision would, or that it was likely to, result in soldiers firing unjustifiably on that day. This observation misses the point. Did the military aid to the maintenance of law and order

---

[11] See the leading case on martial law in Ireland during the civil war in 1920: *Egan v Kennedy* [1921] IR 265, 271 per O'Connor MR and at 279: 'I may be unduly hampering the military authority in their effort to establish peace and order in this distracted country; but I have before me the words of Cockburn CJ in the *Jamaica Case* [1868] Finlason's Report, which were aptly quoted by Mr Healy KC in *Allen's Case* [1921] 2 IR 244: "There are considerations more important even than shortening the temporary duration of an insurrection. Among them are the eternal and immutable principles of justice, principles which can never be violated without lasting detriment to the true interest and well-being of a civilized community"'.

in the Province encompass the potential deployment of the paratroopers `(who were not part of the residential Army force), irrespective of any use of weaponry? Might it not have simply made a finding about the command over the paratroopers, armed or unarmed? In one passage (at 4.8), Lord Saville would seem to put a gloss on the nature of the aid of his troops and whether they were legitimately employed in the 'arrest operation'. He stated that

> 'there is to our minds a significant difference between the risk of soldiers using excessive physical violence when dispersing crowds or *trying to arrest rioters* [italics supplied] and the risk that they would use lethal weapons without justification. We have concluded that General Ford had no reason to believe and did not believe that the risk of soldiers of 1 PARA firing unjustifiably during the course of an arrest operation was such that it was inappropriate for that reason for him to use them for such an operation'.

Accepting the correctness of the latter attitude adopted by General Ford, was he not nevertheless answerable for, at least, authorising the use of paratroopers? Again, the question is posed: would the Inquiry be bound to indicate whether such use of paratroopers was blameworthy? Did not military action breach the system of military aid to the civil power? In this respect the relative powers of arrest in the soldiers and the police was highly relevant to the question of the matters under the heading of 'arrest powers of the soldiers'. This aspect of the service of the military system in the form of the arrest operation was fundamentally to be determined by the absence of the constitutional power in the Army to effect any arrest of a citizen engaged in a matter of civil disorder. Uniquely, the power of any officer to arrest a citizen in Northern Ireland was highly relevant. General Ford committed an error of judgment, but nothing more.

## Arrest Powers of Soldiers

The introduction of internment on 9 August 1971, followed by reactive bouts of civil disturbance on the streets of Derry, provided a curious effect on the control of law and order. Do soldiers in the Province possess the power of policemen to arrest members of the civilian population? And, if not, what was the responsibility of the army commanders to that deficit in their operations? The law provided a recent answer.

During military operations on 18 August 1971 to remove barricades in part of Derry, soldiers encountered a crowd sitting on the ground in an attempt to obstruct further removal of barriers. The crowd included two Northern Ireland MPs, John Hume and Ivan Cooper, together with other prominent citizens. They were arrested by an army officer for remaining in an assembly of more than three persons after having been ordered to disperse. On 8 September 1971 John Hume MP and four others were convicted by two resident magistrates of the offence under regulations made pursuant to the Special Powers Act in the Province, and each was fined £25. A challenge to the High Court by way of judicial review was ultimately successful on 23 February 1972.[12]

The timetable of the proceedings, leading up to the quashing of the convictions by the Lord Chief Justice of Northern Ireland, Lord Lowry, and Justices Gibson and O'Donnell, is important when related to the threat to the Army's ability (or rather inability, as the law stood) to exercise its arrest powers:

25/26 November 1971

Leave to apply for order of certiorari applied for.

29 November 1971

Leave to apply for certiorari was granted by Mr Justice Jones in chambers. Home Office officials were made aware of the legal challenge to the army's powers of arrest.

12 December 1971

Notice of Motion 1971 No 129 lodged in the High Court for hearing on 11 January 1972. Service was executed on the Crown Solicitor.

11/12 January 1972

Case of *Hume v Londonderry Justices* held in the Divisional Court before Sir Robert Lowry CJ, Gibson and O'Donnell JJ. Judgment reserved.

10 February 1972

Mr John MacDermott QC, a legal adviser to the Attorney-General's office in Belfast (later a Lord Justice of Appeal), wrote to Mr Tony Hetherington, legal secretary to the UK Attorney-General in London, advising him of impending judgment. Mr MacDermott expressed a local fear of an adverse ruling, as a result of which 'the Army [would] become impotent as an aid to the civil authority'.

23 February 1972

Judgment handed down, quashing convictions of Hume and others.

23/24 February 1972

Northern Ireland Act 1972 passed through all stages of the Parliamentary process at Westminster, retrospectively validating the acts of army officers arresting persons under the Special Powers Act.

A fortnight before Bloody Sunday, instructions (emanating from the Chief Constable of the RUC, with the approval of the Director of Operations Committee) were issued to senior police officers of the RUC and all brigades concerning the enforcement of the ban on processions made by the Minister of Home Affairs in the Stormont administration prohibiting the holding of all public processions on any public highway. The instructions, dated 19 January 1972, told the police and

---

[12] *Hume and others v Londonderry Justices* [1972] NI 91.

the army what action was to be taken whenever the ministerial prohibition was being defied, and indicated what powers the Army (if called on by the civilian authorities) would exercise. By that time, or shortly thereafter, Chief Superintendent Lagan, Head of N Division of the RUC (which covered the city of Derry) was told informally that NICRA was organising an anti-internment march on 30 January 1972, in blatant defiance of the ban on marches. And the military were aware of the impending march, if only through the meetings of the Joint Security Committee, a body set up by the Northern Ireland Government to deal with security issues.

Paragraph 6 of the instructions provided:

> The powers of arrest under the Public Order Act [1951 to 1970] should be exercised at the time [of the defiance of the ban] if practicable, by the RUC. Uniformed and plain-clothed police must in any case identify as many persons as possible taking part in the procession and note their degree of involvement. Arrests under the Public Order Act will not be carried out by the Army but should it be necessary for the Army to make any arrests they will do so under Regulation 11 of the Special Powers Act on suspicion of committing acts prejudicial to the peace or of having committed an offence against the Regulations.

The author of the instructions no doubt relied upon section 7 of the Civil Authorities (Special Powers) Act 1922, as amended by the Civil Authorities (Special Powers) Act 1933, which provided that 'any person authorised by the civil authority, or any police constable or member of any of His Majesty's forces on duty' had the power to arrest people for criminal offences or breaches of regulations made under the 1922 Act. (The schedule to the Act conferred further powers upon members of the Armed Forces.)

A week earlier, on 11 and 12 January 1972, the High Court of Northern Ireland (Lord Lowry CJ, Gibson and O'Donnell JJ) had reserved judgment in a challenge by five persons against their conviction on 8 September 1971 by the Londonderry Justices of unlawful assembly; the challenge, by way of certiorari, was that regulations conferring powers, *inter alia* of arrest, on the British armed forces were *ultra vires* the Government of Ireland Act 1920. That Imperial Act, the Constitution of Northern Ireland, established the Northern Ireland Parliament at Stormont, giving it authority to make 'laws for the peace, order and good government of' the Province, but, by section 4 of the 1920 Act, provided that it should not have 'power to make laws in respect of the following matters in particular, namely … (3) the Navy, the Army, the Air Force, the Territorial Army, or any other naval, military, or air force, or the defence of the realm, or any other naval, military or air force matter …' Judgment was given on 23 February 1972, in favour of the applicants, that the Special Powers Act was *ultra vires* the Government of Ireland Act 1920.[13] On the basis that the law was always as stated by the High Court, the Army did

---

[13] *Hume and others v Londonderry Justices* [1972] NI 91.

not possess the power of arrest on 30 January 1972, either under the Public Order Act or the Special Powers Act. The purported arrests of civilian marchers on that day were thus unlawful, until the passing of the Northern Ireland Act 1972 on 24 February 1972 retrospectively validated the supposed powers exercised by the military under the legislation of the Stormont administration.

The Crown immediately obtained leave to appeal from the High Court in Belfast to the House of Lords, but the British government thought that an appeal was not a practical possibility; the Lord Chancellor, Lord Hailsham, said that 'we could not leave these powers unused for as long as would be necessary to hear the Appeal'.[14] The decision to challenge the High Court's ruling in the final court of appeal was thus rejected in favour of a Bill rushed through all its parliamentary stages in one day—to be precise, seven hours and eleven minutes—not merely negating the court ruling but legislating retrospectively. The Bill provided:

> The limitations imposed by paragraph (3) of section 4(1) of the Government of Ireland Act 1920 on the powers of the Parliament of Northern Ireland to make laws shall not have effect, and shall be deemed never to have had effect to preclude the inclusion in laws made by that Parliament for the peace, order or good government of Northern Ireland of all provision done by them, and shall be deemed never to have precluded the conferment on them by, or under or in pursuance of any such law of powers, authorities, privileges or immunities in relation to the preservation of the peace or the maintenance of order in Northern Ireland.

The government's view was that the Bill had a limited purpose. The Lord Chancellor described the Bill as 'the extremely narrow as well as extremely technical nature of the legislation we are now passing'. He pointed to three things illustrating that description:[15]

> We are not validating anything which was not invalidated this morning. *If any acts were done illegally outside the powers conferred upon them by the Minister, they are still illegal and they would still give rise to an action in the courts*: they would still give rise to an action for civil damages, where civil damages are proper, and they would still give rise to criminal proceedings if a criminal offence is committed. Nothing of that kind is validated. Secondly, the particular convictions which were quashed by the High Court will remain quashed if this legislation is passed. This is because, although leave to appeal was obtained, we shall abandon our appeal if this Bill is given legislative force. Therefore those who gained the advantage of the judgment this morning will be allowed to keep it for all time without interference.

NICRA made this point (unavailingly) to the Saville Inquiry, while (as at the time the Convention was not part of the national law of the United Kingdom) acknowledging that the question 'might reasonably have not occurred to legal authorities in 1971/2'.[16] It could not be said that the ruling of the High Court on 23 February

---

[14] HL Deb 23 February 1972, vol 328, col 624.
[15] HL Deb 23 February 1972, vol 328, col 624 (italics supplied).
[16] Report of the Saville Inquiry, para 195.26.

1972 was entirely unexpected, since the legal powers of the Army had been known to be questionable for many years, most recently in 1969 when British troops were sent to Northern Ireland. As long ago as 1936 a commission of inquiry set up by the National Council of Civil Liberties (now called Liberty) had commented on the provisions. It said:[17]

> It is curious that parts of the Special Powers Act purport to confer powers upon members of the armed forces. The title of the legislation 'Civil Authorities Act' appears to exclude the exercise of 'Special Powers' by other than civil authorities an assumption which is borne out by the limits of the Home Minister's powers of delegation ie to any officer of police. But in this respect the Schedule travels far beyond the Act to which it is appended by specifically empowering the military authorities to exercise rights and perform duties which from the purport of the Act itself should be strictly confined to civilians.

The 1936 NCCL commission of inquiry, which was composed of Mr Edward Aylmer Digby QC, Miss Margery Fry, Mr William McKeag and Mr Edward Lancelot Mallalieu (the last two had been Liberal MPs from 1931–35), with Mr Neil (later Mr Justice) Lawson as secretary, was reviewed in October 1972 in the light of subsequent events. It noted that the 1936 report had been reprinted many times, 'most recently in 1972', and proceeded to comment on the subsequent legislative changes that had affected the situation. It stated:[18]

> ...the Northern Ireland Act 1972 has dealt with an objection raised by the 1936 NCCL Commission and since upheld by the Northern Ireland High Court in *R v Hume and others*, that the Regulations were *ultra vires* the Stormont Government in so far as they purport to confer powers and immunities upon the armed forces. The Northern Ireland Act 1972 retrospectively amended the Government of Ireland Act 1920 to legitimise regulations which, as legal academics had for many years in Ireland taught their students, were invalid.

Whatever may have been the legal advice to government in 1972, that legal opinion could not have been regarded as decisive; indeed it had been problematical ever since 1936. But it was part of the everyday activities of Northern Ireland.

The statement in paragraph 6 of the police instructions, asserting boldly the Army's powers to arrest under the Special Powers Act, was questionable, in the light of the hearings a week before in the High Court in Belfast. Even if the conclusion is that the government was entitled to rely on advice from its own lawyers, the doubt about the continuing constitutionality of the military operation to deal with marches should have given pause for thought to the military authorities and the Joint Security Committee in the days leading up to Bloody Sunday.

The proceedings against John Hume and his colleagues for public order offences in mid-1971 (and the certiorari proceedings begun in late 1971) directly involved the power of arrest by the armed forces acting in aid of the police. At the very least,

---

[17] At p 15–16.
[18] para 4, p 3.

the relevant government departments might have reconsidered carefully the constitutionality of the powers of the armed forces in the light of those proceedings. Those advising the government must have been actively pondering, ever since 29 November 1971 when the High Court in Belfast granted the applicants leave to apply for an order of certiorari, the likely outcome of the legal challenge. At the conclusion of the full hearing of the application on 12 January 1972, the parties are likely to have received some indication, from the course of the oral arguments by counsel and the judicial interventions from the Bench, about what the likely outcome of the application was. Whatever the respective counsel for the parties may have been communicating to their clients about the likely outcome, it must be assumed that government, both at Whitehall and Stormont, were actively considering what steps might be needed to respond to a judgment adverse to the Crown's contention that the powers conferred on the Army by section 7 of the Special Powers Act were *intra vires* the Government of Ireland Act 1920. Apart from discussions between the two governments, the legal advisers to the Chief Constable and to the Army Command, respectively, will surely have been consulted in the drafting of the Police Instructions of 19 January 1972.

Assuming that the Northern Ireland Act 1972 was, and is, a valid piece of legislation, two questions arise. What action, if any, should have been taken by the military authorities in conjunction with the RUC in the days before Bloody Sunday to satisfy themselves that paragraph 6 of the police instructions of 19 January 1972 accurately stated the constitutional position about the Army's arrest powers, having regard to the hearing on 11 and 12 January in the High Court in Belfast and the clear indication of the Court's likely decision? A second question, that might reasonably not have occurred to legal authorities in 1971/2, but is relevant to a historical view of the position, is whether the Northern Ireland Act 1972 was compatible with Article 7 of the European Convention on Human Rights. (One MP in the debate on the 1972 Bill, Mr Leslie Huckfield, thought that retrospective legislation 'on matters like this goes against the very grain' of the Convention[19] and the issue came before the European Court of Human Rights on 3 March 1972.)

It was fully recognised, both in Whitehall and at Stormont, that it was primarily for the Joint Security Committee in Northern Ireland to decide on the tactics which the security forces should adopt for dealing with NICRA's anti-internment march scheduled for 30 January 1972. The Joint Security Committee, with the Prime Minister, Mr Brian Faulkner, in the chair, met on 13 January 1972, the day after the High Court of Northern Ireland had reserved its judgment in *Hume v Londonderry Justices*. Present at the meeting were Lord Kilclooney (then Mr John Taylor) as Minister of State for the Ministry of Home Affairs, the GOC (General Tuzo), the Chief Constable (Sir Graham Shillington) and the UK Representative (Mr Howard Smith). The purpose of the meeting was to agree to a renewal for a

---

[19] HC Deb 23 February 1972, vol 831, col 1414.

further year of the ban on marches beyond the expiry date of 8 February 1972, yet there appears to have been no reference made to the potentially adverse result to the Crown's assertion that the Army possessed ample powers to enforce the provisions of the Special Powers Act. A modification of existing procedures, in a memorandum of 5 January 1972, which was before the Committee on 13 January 1972, contained a suggestion that 'on-the-spot' arrests of ringleaders, including perhaps well-known citizens, and other marchers, might be made; this would normally be done by the RUC under the Public Order Act, 'but the Army would participate if any violence were offered'. If the impact of the High Court hearing on 11/12 January 1972 could not reasonably have been assimilated by 13 January, the issue could hardly have escaped notice, and serious discussion, a fortnight later when the Joint Security Committee, chaired by John Taylor MP in the absence of the Prime Minister, met to consider Operational Order 2/72 (the 'scoop-up' operation) for dealing with the Derry march on 30 January 1972. The minutes of the meeting disclose a discussion about 'serious difficulties and security action [which] will be primarily an Army operation' without any reference being made to the constitutional powers of the Army to effect arrests under the Special Powers Act. Lord Kilclooney, in his evidence to the Saville Inquiry on 14 March 2002, said that he had no knowledge of the case involving John Hume and his colleagues. Nor indeed was there even the presence of any legal adviser, even if only for the purpose of informing the Committee of the possible outcome of the High Court proceedings. No reference appears to have been made on that occasion to the instructions, dated 19 January 1972, from the Chief Constable to Divisional Commanders.

The absence of any legal advice to the relevant authorities in the days immediately preceding Bloody Sunday constituted a failure to act administratively in an appropriate manner. In terms of ombudsmanry, this was, classically, an act of maladministration.

## The Inquiry's Response

Lord Saville dealt with this topic in 27 paragraphs of his report. Unlike other issues that were left unaddressed, the question of arrest powers for the police is fully addressed. The conclusion is:

> 195.18 To our minds, in view of the matters considered in the previous paragraphs, *we consider that any advice tendered before Bloody Sunday could only, at the highest, have been to the effect that there was a serious risk that the High Court of Northern Ireland would hold that the regulations under which John Hume and others were arrested, and by extension other similar provisions made under the Special Powers Act, were invalid.*[20]

> 195.19 Had such advice been given, the authorities (ultimately the United Kingdom Government), would have been faced with a number of choices. They could have waited for

---

[20] Italics supplied.

the judgment and then, if it was adverse, sought to appeal to the House of Lords. They could, pending the decision of the High Court of Northern Ireland, have ceased to use members of the Armed Forces in aid of the civil power in Northern Ireland, at least in circumstances where such use depended upon the validity of the regulations. They could have rushed through legislation validating the regulations, as indeed they were to do in the aftermath of the decision in the Hume case.

195.20 The first of these choices, an appeal to the House of Lords, which in any event might have been unsuccessful, would have taken time, and in the period between the High Court decision and the conclusion of the appeal the Armed Forces could hardly have been permitted to act as though the impugned regulations were valid. The second choice would have meant that the same situation would have arisen even before the High Court of Northern Ireland had ruled. In the situation as it obtained in Northern Ireland at the time, the result in either of these cases would have been that *the Armed Forces would have been substantially hampered in their task of aiding the civil power in Northern Ireland.*[21] To our minds it would not have been unreasonable for the relevant decision makers to conclude that this would amount to an unacceptable state of affairs that precluded the adoption of either of these two approaches.

Even if that is the right answer, it does not face the point that General Ford might reasonably have decided *not* to effect the 'arrest operation' by paratroopers, over and above the policing of the march. Since the 'arrest operation' designedly involved the act of unrest, General Ford might have been led to forgo an important legal power. Is a plan by a military commander to direct that a company of paratroopers might be used to effect arrests of rioting hooligans at the end of a civil rights march, policed by resident regiments in the Province, a 'military operation'? The question was not given a reasoned answer.

# Legality of the Ban

In a public inquiry to investigate the circumstances of deaths of people killed in the course of a civil rights march, ostensibly banned by the relevant authority, what could be more desirable or just than a claim by the organisers of the march that the ban was in fact unlawful? Even if (as was the case) the citizenry of Derry and the authorities policing the event acted on the basis that the march was illegal, many leading citizens—such as Bishop Daly—viewed the organisers' decision prior to 30 January 1972, to demonstrate in defiance of the internment introduced in August 1971, as a manifestation of the fundamental right of assembly and procession due to any citizen. Lord Widgery in his earlier Bloody Sunday Inquiry of April 1972 had concluded that the Northern Ireland Civil Rights Association, the organiser of the march, had been found to be blameworthy for the deaths because

---

[21] Italics supplied.

it had brought thousands of its supporters onto the streets of Derry, knowing of the real risk to life and limb from the security forces. That explicit finding deserved refutation, which Lord Saville provided. His report said:[22]

> In our view the organisers of the civil rights march bear no responsibility for the deaths and injuries on Bloody Sunday. Although those who organised the march must have realised that there was probably going to be trouble from rioters, they had no reason to believe, and did not believe, that this was likely to result in death or injury from unjustified firing of soldiers.

Given that resounding vindication of the organisers of the march from any foresight of the consequences of the march, and from any responsibility for the ensuing tragedy, it would logically follow that a claim of illegality by virtue of the ministerial ban on marches should have been addressed. Yet the report declines even to meet, let alone consider the validity of the claim. The report states:[23]

> At this Inquiry it was submitted that the circumstances in which the Northern Ireland Government came to introduce a ban on marches in August 1971 raised the question of whether the ban fell outside the provisions of the Public Order Act and violated Articles 10 and 11 of the European Convention on Human Rights, on the grounds that it was introduced by the Government of Northern Ireland, not for genuine security reasons, but as the price to be paid for the agreement of the United Kingdom Government to internment. It is neither necessary nor desirable in this report to express a view on these matters, which are essentially questions of law, since we have no evidence to suggest that any of those taking part in, or seeking to stop, the march on Bloody Sunday acted otherwise than in the belief that it had been legally banned, and since it is far from certain that all the relevant evidence, materials and arguments have been put before us.

The argument that was advanced before Lord Saville had been presented in an article in *The Political Quarterly* in 2006,[24] to which reference is made in the report. The argument, put shortly, was this: on 5 August 1971 the Prime Minister of Northern Ireland, Mr Brian Faulkner (who died in 1977) came to London with his adviser and met with the British Prime Minister, Mr Edward Heath, and cabinet members. The essence of the meeting was to discuss Mr Faulkner's clear desire to bring in internment as the only solution to the worsening situation of accentuated civil disobedience and violent disorder in the Province. Mr Faulkner needed the assent of the British government to exercise his statutory power to ban, at his discretion, any march in the Province (or parts of the Province). The necessity for agreement from the British government was that the act of internment—in fact, detention without trial—would violate the European Convention on Human Rights, and as such required a derogation from the United Kingdom's obligation under the Convention. The British Prime Minister was finally persuaded to

---

[22] At para 4.33.
[23] At para 8.48.
[24] Vol 77, pp 227–37.

agree to internment, so long as Mr Faulkner, simultaneously introducing internment, coincidentally banned *all* marches in the Province, under separate statutory
power, for the duration of the internment. On 9 August 1971 the government
in Northern Ireland announced the exercise of these directly-linked powers. In
terms of the principles of administrative law, as developed by the courts of law,
Mr Faulkner was bound to perform the agreement made with the British government; he thereby fettered his statutory discretion when exercising his power to
ban marches.

The minutes of the Cabinet meeting of 5 August 1971, together with evidence
from Sir Edward Heath, Lord Carrington and officials from the Ministry of
Defence at Whitehall (all of whom gave evidence, to the like effect, to the Saville
Inquiry), demonstrated that Mr Faulkner had no alternative, willy-nilly, but to
ban all marches. The ban itself was thus illegal. This refusal to consider an issue
relevant to the events of 30 January 1972 was a glaring instance of a classic failure
of a public inquiry to appreciate the essential primacy to determine how and why
the deaths occurred, and what action had been taken that led to the tragic killings.
The march which was at the core of the day's events was said to be illegal, in which
case the organisers of the march would be entitled not only to claim a moral right
to engage in civil disobedience, but also to demonstrate that, under the rule of
law, the authorities had misunderstood the law that appeared to authorise their
administrative powers.

Attendance at the march organised publicly by the Northern Ireland Civil Rights
Association in Derry on 30 January 1972, personally and peacefully unarmed, was
another demonstration ostensibly in blatant defiance of the ban on all marches
in the Province since August 1971. But it called for a rather more sophisticated
attitude by the enforcers of the law. Many sympathisers with the aims of NICRA
(who had themselves been active in this epoch of such demonstrations), however,
genuinely felt that the cross-community ban on all marches, which also affected
Orange and Unionist marches, was intended to provide a breathing space in the
volatile political situation. The existence of the ban failed to dissuade the organisers of the march from going ahead, knowing that it had the support of the local
police commander. It was thought by some that this was not just a march about
civil rights, but something akin to civil disorder, even outright civil war. It was
seen, not unjustifiably, as an assertion by the Catholic community and others of
an outright hostility against the majority, Protestant, community. How vital, then,
that a nakedly political judgment should be enforced by the legal system, a system
that should give full play to the inherent freedom of peaceful assembly. Unarmed
and managed by stewards, the march should have alerted the Army authorities and
the RUC to an expression of civil disobedience of a non-violent nature. It was not
tantamount to war-like action, but simply an act of civil disobedience, warranting
arrest, but no more.

Such a thoughtful appreciation of the projected event would undoubtedly have
been a deciding factor. The unlawful action of Brian Faulkner, fettering his statutory discretion on 9 August 1971 to sanction the march and excluding police from

the marches with only the regular armed forces in residence in Northern Ireland was definitionally optimistic. The ban could have been easily maintained without the excrescence of an armed company of paratroopers in place, in anticipation of disruptive behaviour by violent hooligans. If only there had been a process of consultation between General Ford and the RUC officers, the legality (or possible illegality) of the decision of August 1971 might have provided a moment's pause, and the killing of innocent people by those responsible for maintaining law and order might have been avoided.

A plausible answer would be to observe that the law of public administration, through the development in the late 1960s of manifest judicial review of ministerial decision-making, was in its forensic infancy. Even more embryonic was the administrative law in Northern Ireland. But the failure of the Saville Report to illuminate the nascent law relating to ministerial powers cannot excuse the disclosure in 2010 of the unlawful ban on marching in 1972.

I favour the remark made by Bishop Daley at the time of the tragic event, 'What else could we do?'. Short of the imposition of martial law, the right to march, violating Article II of the European Convention on Human Rights (a factor that may not have been known to the organisers of the march of 30 January 1972) is still a civil right. Banned or unbanned, was it still less than a civil rights march?

The claim made 30 years after the event that the march was not illegal was not hypothetical. It had a real meaning for those who claimed the fundamental right to march in defiance of the ban. Doubtless, the provision was universally regarded as lawful. But the best that can be said about the authority was that it was only apparently lawful. Moreover, the Bloody Sunday Inquiry was the last opportunity for an authoritative ruling on the legality of the ban and of the march, and, if further evidence was needed, surely it was the Inquiry's duty to adduce it—at some time during the 12½ years. The opportunity was sadly missed. Was not the legality of the march a crucial aspect of a public inquiry investigating the events that followed tragically from political decisions of ministers made in England and Northern Ireland?

# Conclusion

Thoroughness was the leitmotif of the Saville Inquiry (effectiveness is what is required above all, as the Council on Tribunals pointedly and primarily advised the Lord Chancellor in 1996). The burden of public funding was unbudgeted and then imposed by its chairman, without due regard to the consequent delay and growing cost. Lord Saville's pursuit of justice to the individual paratroopers involved inevitably a vast cost to public funds. When he appeared before the Northern Ireland Affairs Committee on 13 October 2010, Lord Saville confirmed that at the start of the Inquiry, 'we had no idea how long that was going to take [official estimates at the outset were 18 months to 2 years], and that is going to be the case with any inquiry of this sort of nature'. He added, pointedly—or should it be, arguably—that the Bloody Sunday Inquiry was not, in fact an inquiry into one incident, '*because we had to look at each individual shooting*, because to do otherwise would be, apart from anything else, grossly unfair to the soldiers concerned'. There, in a nutshell, is Lord Saville's answer to the imposition of the 27 paratroopers' collective responsibility and his profound concern for each individual soldier's liability. The cost of £200m lay in the fundamental concept of fairness. Legalism had to prevail. Was it fair to the concerned public?

There would have been nothing unfair about the Saville Inquiry proceeding to find that the paratroopers were collectively responsible for the fatal shootings. There would be no legal effect from such a finding; there was only the possibility that the findings of fact about how that collectiveness pointed inferentially to individual culpability, in which case ordinary criminal proceedings might ensue. Much potentially in November 2015 has occurred by the arrest and charge by the Police Service of Northern Ireland (PSNI) of one of the 27 paratroopers; other soldiers might similarly face criminal proceedings. On 17 December 2015 the High Court held that the paratroopers could not be ordered to attend for investigation by the PSNI. Only then would the Saville Inquiry's report be followed by formal police investigation and the possible trials of individuals. Until such time, any criminal justice system is prospectively inapt ('sterile of legal effect'); Saville's report possesses valuable information for ministerial authorities, as well as historical interest of mammoth proportions—and future inquiries must never be so costly. Stripped of all the relevant factors that distorted the methodology, the fundamental flaw was Lord Saville's adherence to the principle of fairness in the adversarial sense, which is entirely inapposite in the inquisitorial system of public inquiries. Was it fair to the public, and not restricted to individual witnesses to the day's events? Lord Saville might gratefully receive as his motto, 'Once a judge, always a judge'. Unfortunately, the public inquiry, being 'sterile of legal effect', is not judicially empowered. It is a function of good government. It incorporates the essence of decision-making in public affairs.

# Part IV

# The Inquiries Act 2005

# 8

## An Analysis of the Act of 2005:
## An Aspect of Public Administration

The Council on Tribunals (later abolished) in July 1996, in its advice to the Lord Chancellor, concluded that it was 'wholly impracticable to attempt to devise a single set of model rules or guidance that will provide for the constitution, procedure and powers of every inquiry'. Such issues, it said, should be addressed by taking into account each inquiry. But it declared that the object must be 'effectiveness [note, not thoroughness], fairness, speed and economy'.[1] The Inquiries Act 2005, however, sets out a uniform system and procedures for all statutory inquiries; it preserves other forms of non-statutory inquiry, such as the Chilcot Inquiry into the Iraq war.

A distinguishing feature of all public inquiries, whether statutory or non-statutory, has been (and still is) the standard of proof required to make good the tribunal's findings of fact and its decision-making. This is all the more so in the absence of an appellate process. The report depends upon the question of whether the standard is that of beyond a reasonable doubt, required before a criminal conviction can be arrived at, or a balance of probability, as in civil trials, but this is inapt for the commissioner(s) to report their conclusions. The standard adopted is similar to any decision that an administrator would be required to make in pursuance of his public duty under the relevant statutory or other power. Here, there was at least a useful precedent from the Bloody Sunday Inquiry. Belatedly, on 11 October 2004, Lord Saville ruled on submissions (themselves tardily made by the soldiers) that, without implying criminal conduct or serious wrongdoing, it was vital that the principle of fairness dictated that it should be similarly applied to their respective cases. He applied a standard of proof for fact-finding in a public inquiry.

So long as the tribunal makes it crystal clear that the degree of confidence or certainty with which it reaches any conclusion as to facts and matters that may

---

[1] The Council on Tribunals was an independent advisory body which was established in 1958 following the Franks Report on Administrative Tribunals and Inquiries. Its functions, which were set out in the Tribunals and Inquiries Act 1992, included keeping under review the constitution and working of a large number of tribunals and advising on administrative procedures relating to certain statutory inquiries. The Council had a Scottish Committee with direct responsibility for supervising tribunals set up under Scottish legislation.

imply or suggest criminality or serious misconduct of any individual (provided always that there is good evidence and reasoning that logically supports the conclusion), there can be no unfairness to anyone nor any reason to limit the tribunal's findings. It is not litigation, but fairness will always dictate that those who might be criticised have been given a proper opportunity to deal with allegations made against them. Where the witness is legally represented during the hearing of evidence of blameworthiness, that opportunity to deal with the criticism is presumed. (The same would apply, *mutatis mutandis*, with those who have been given 'core participant' status.) Where, since the Inquiries Act 2005, there is no application of the Six Salmon Principles, the procedure for warning witnesses of potential criticism in the provisional report becomes operative (this is dealt with in chapter 11 dealing with safeguards for witnesses).

A number of factors surrounding the impact of the Human Rights Act 1998 and the dialogue following the Scott Report in 1997 on the status of the witnesses to events under inquiry prompted considerations of social policies of the Labour administration that triumphed at the election of 1997. Faithful to the tradition of political dissociation from judicial activity, on the ground that the Executive should not intrude on the judicial power of the courts, politicians quietly fumed at the mounting cost to public funds of the Inquiry. More pertinent comments focused on the disproportionate involvement of the legal profession in processing the testimony of witnesses; and the legal profession sensed its forensic function in the task of inquisition was threatened. The public debate was critical (mostly in the moderate language of the late Lord Howe of Aberavon) of the way the Scott inquiry had dispensed with legal representation in the hearings, and felt unhappy at the method of safeguarding witnesses who were liable to blameworthiness in the impending report. The aftermath of the Scott inquiry provided the stimulus of legislation which prompted the unsung parliamentary caution of the first decade of the twenty-first century. The uncontroversial nature of the legislation reflected the general desire for a simple framework. If the Inquiries Act 2005 avoided the vagaries of the parliamentary process, the legislation was a major piece of reform, much applauded by the House of Lords in the select committee's study of the first years of its functioning, leaving only the delegated legislation of the Inquiry Rules 2006 to require further review, still awaited in 2016.

What then in practice was reformed? If the burdensome factor of the costs was to be effectively tackled, the restriction on the use of witnesses with their multiple counsel clocking up their hours of public remuneration was the prime target. The novel provision of the 'core participant' to the interested witness, at the discretion of the tribunal, undoubtedly constrained the costly attendance of the examiners and cross-examiners. The absence of long-windedness (even controlled by the chairman) has been the most notable sign of the public inquiry. But it is the structure of the legislation that, it strikes the commentator, has the overriding effect. If, ever since 1921, the public inquiry had not in any sense been a part of the legal system that enforces the ensuing liability for the event, then as what sort of animal can the commission of inquiry be described?

The prime actor in the public inquiry is the sponsoring minister, with his absolute power to frame the inquiry's terms of reference, which reflect the questions that politicians and policy would seem to reflect the minister's wish. And his power to determine the acceptance or not of the report and its recommendations is determinative of the verdict. Stripped of the details of legalism, it is maintained that the inquisition has shed itself of the adversarial process of judicial fact-finding. The ministerial power demonstrates that his political act of outsourcing the investigation of the public concern is in pursuance of his ministerial duties to administer in his departmental office a part of good government. Of the three arms of government in a democratic society the public inquiry fits more neatly under the rubric of public administration. It is not judicial, in any sense other than that a person with pronounced qualities of judging human behaviour in an orderly fashion is instinctively qualified to provide a valuable form of assessing both documentary and oral testimony in the fact-finding process. Overall, fairness is as much an attribute of someone without judicial qualifications as it is in his judge-counterpart. Tested regularly, the maxim for chairmanship is 'horses for courses'. While effectiveness, fairness, speed and economy have contributed to reform, the question of fairness reigns supreme.

What are the singular attributes of a commission of inquiry that proclaim it as an outcrop of public administration, and that the report of the inquiry is devoid of any legal power (only in the procedure can there be any judicial oversight)?

The commission is the commissioner, whether or not he happens to be (or to have been) a judge exercising the judicial oath of independence and impartiality. Second, the commission performs its task as the terms of reference convey. The minister seeks to have answers to his question. The commissioner finds the facts and expresses his conclusions. The minister receives the report for publication; he may delegate that function. But the minister is the master of publication. If he wishes, he can indicate the degree to which he accepts the findings. He is entitled to say thank you, and decline to do anything more. Since the Inquiries Act 2005, there is no requirement of parliamentary approach to the establishment of an inquiry. Only with the judiciary, in conformity with its power to review a ministerial decision, is there any surveillance—except public opinion. Public inquiries are part of the administration of peace, order and good government.

Lord Saville's approach to the methodology of the Salmon Commission is exemplified by his response to the proposed legislature of the 2005 Act. On 26 January 2005 he was asked, in correspondence with the government preparing the legislation, whether he would be prepared to accept an appointment to an inquiry that was subject to a provision which gave the minister sponsoring the inquiry a power to impose restrictions at any time before the end of the inquiry at the attendance of the inquiry, or on the disclosure or publication, especially in any case where the conduct of the authorities is in question.

I cite verbatim Lord Saville's answer. He said:

I take the view that this provision makes a very serious inroad into the independence of any Inquiry; and is likely to damage or destroy public confidence in the inquiry and its find-

ings, especially in the case where the conduct of the authorities might be in question ...
[I] would not be prepared to be appointed as a member of an inquiry that was subject
to a provision of this kind ... It is for the inquiry panel itself to determine these matters,
subject of course to the right of those concerned to challenge in court any ruling
[or finding that the panel might make or refuse to make].

These remarks indicate a conflation of the essential duty to conduct the inquiry
with the crucial independence to judge the evidence. The degree to which an
enquiry secures the public confidence of independence and impartiality of the
chairman and the panellists has nothing to do with the provisions of the 2005
Act which necessarily divest the method of evaluating the substantive evidence of
the witnesses. Fairness, in ensuring the public's confidence, stems predominantly
from the inquiry's conduct of the evidence, rather than the existence of procedural
powers set out in the legislation.

Once the minister has ordered an inquiry to be conducted by someone other
than from among the civil servants of his or her department (whether it is to be
conducted in public or in private session), the inquiry is a public inquiry. The procedure is at that point a matter for the inquirer; his or her independence, the conduct of the proceedings and the submission to the minister of the inquiry report.
As Sir Brian Kerr (now a Justice of the Supreme Court) explained in 2006 in *Re
Wright* in the Court of Appeal in Northern Ireland:[2]

> If the Secretary of State has power to bring an inquiry to an end, does that ineluctably
> compromise its independence? We do not believe that it does. The opportunity to stop
> the inquiry does not have a direct impact on its independence. It may affect its usefulness
> in that it halts the investigation on which the inquiry is embarked, but it does not alter
> the autonomy of the inquiry while it is taking place.

Independence is, necessarily, maintained in the quality of the published report.
That will depend on a proper analysis of the verdict on the fact-finding process
and the reasoning advanced for that verdict. Any expression of opinion on the
issues of social and political policy will always be subjected to opposing views.
Such a division of opinion does not invalidate the inherent correctness of the
facts as found by the inquiry; the data evinced in the material accumulated in the
inquiry process is present to be publicly observable and adjudicated upon by the
reasonable reader. Independence of the commission of inquiry is, at most, a relative concept. Sir Brian Kerr explains at paragraph 30 how the public inquiry under
the 2005 legislation is conducted contextually. The same principle applies to the
non-statutory form of public inquiry.

---

[2] *Re Wright* [2007] NICA 24, at para 29.

# 9

# The Chairing of Commissions:
# Horses for Courses

The Salmon report in 1966 recommended, in its advocacy for legalism to prevail, that a tribunal of inquiry must be chaired by a person holding high judicial office. Lord Salmon considered that 'apart from assurance that having a judge as chairman gives to the public that the inquiry is being conducted impartially and efficiently ... it ensures that the powers of the tribunal will be exercised judicially'. But in 1996 the Lord Chancellor, Lord Mackay, stated that the British practice was only to use judges 'rather sparingly' to conduct inquiries. The figures from the time suggest otherwise. Of the notable inquiries set up between 1990 and 2004, 58% were chaired by a serving judge (the percentage goes up to 64.5% if retired judges are included). The penchant for judicial chairmen was still marked, while in a distinguished address in 2004[1] Mr (now Lord) Justice Beatson argued forcibly to an Israeli audience (where the legislation provides for a judge to be the chairman) that judges, where contemplated for hearing inquiries, should be used sparingly whenever sensitive or political issues were the subject under investigation. In the Inquiries Act 2005, Parliament did not single out the judge as a primary person to act as a commissioner of inquiry. It left the selection of the inquiry's panellists to the sponsoring minister.

Apart from the sponsoring minister's duty to consult with the head of the proposed chairman's judiciary when seeking to ask a judge to conduct a commission of inquiry, there is nothing in the Inquiries Act 2005 that differentiates between commissioners, whatever their daily occupations may be. This sensible safeguard against any compulsory use of judicial manpower recognises that a judge's expertise and experience point to their preferment to head an investigation of an issue that concerns the public. That much is indeed borne out by the fact that since the legislation almost all of the inquiries have been conducted by retired members of the higher judiciary.

A commissioner of inquiry acknowledges that, by statute now, he is beholden to the sponsoring minister. If that makes him an emanation of the administration by the minister's department of state, he might like to be treated simply as an ad hoc extension of ministerial accountability. But to call the commission of inquiry

---

[1] Reproduced at (2005) *LQR* 221.

(which, palpably, is not a court of law or a tribunal) *sui generis* is to deploy a Latinist phrase that hardly qualifies as a public institution with an English nomenclature. The legal autonomy of the inquiry lies within the statute in which Parliament confers control on ministers of the Crown. Without doubt, the attributes of the legally qualified practitioner on the Bench rate highly in the minds of those who seek those attributes. The process of fact-finding in an analysis and absorption of the often massive documentation is the hallmark of judicial action. It is the question of the value judgment of the relevant systems and services in public administration that give rise to wider considerations than mere decision-making which is often treated as political or as involving public policies.

Whenever a commission of inquiry is appointed to investigate an issue of a public disaster or a social scandal there is a strong inclination to select a member of the judiciary to chair the inquiry, emphasising that the reason for a public inquiry is the breadth of the topic under surveillance: it is *not* litigation but investigation. The apparent reason is simple. Judges form a revered group in British society. They are privileged more for their acknowledged skill at testing the credibility of witnesses and their reliability in retelling their testimony. But above all, they are regarded as independent and impartial of the executive form of government, a view which they rightly treasure and foster. An editorial in *The Lancet* in 1950 extolled specifically to professionals the supreme status in society of the family doctor, 'unless they sit on the judge's bench'. Occupationally, the role of judges is to act under the judicial oath of impartiality to the litigating parties. It is part and parcel of the concept of the judicial distancing from political influences. It bears out the familiar principle of the 'separation of powers'. A cogent analysis of the ideological foundations of the separation of powers but can be found in the essay by Professor Judith Shklar on *Legalism*.[2] Legalism, she proclaims, stresses not only the differences between law and politics, but also the profound belief that the features of litigation in a legal system (with the unique permit of precedent and the search for certainty and continuity) are intrinsically virtuous, rendering the law superior as distinct from politics. The classical view was expressed by her. She wrote:

> ... there appears to be virtually unanimous agreement that law and politics must be kept apart as much as possible in theory no less than in practice. The divorce of law from politics is, to be sure, designed to prevent arbitrariness, and that is why there is so little argument about its necessity. However, ideologically, legalism does not stop there. Politics is regarded not only as something apart from law, but as inferior to law. Law aims at justice, while politics looks only to expediency. The former is neutral and objective, the latter the uncontrolled child of competing ideologies.

While there are reasonable grounds for keeping politics out of the legal process, judicial independence is fundamentally a valuable asset in any democratic system,

---

[2] (Harvard University Press, 1964) 111. Also see Drewry, 'Judges and Political Inquiries: Harnessing a Myth' (1975) 23 *Political Science* 49.

even if the development of judicial review since the 1970s has clouded the separation of powers and regards the three arms of democratic government as acting in harmony, if functionally not harnessed. But any distinction between law and politics operates only so long as the judge acts as a judge in litigation. When the judge discards his judicial robe in favour of the chairmanship of an inquiry, he becomes a valued civil servant in the same role as any legally unqualified commissioner of inquiry. Chairmen of public inquiries no doubt adopt the same approach procedurally. But does he perform the same role in reporting the findings of his inquiry—his judgment on public affairs?

# A Sparing of Judicial Talent

Nevertheless, there is a real point in the observations of Lord Justice Beatson, that in inquiries which touch upon controversial political and social policies, the judicial chairman should be restrictively isolated. The fear is that observations in the report that intrude upon political issues might jeopardise the vaunted principle of independence. Better to leave political and social issues to those who understand the relevant politics and social issues. Therein lies the key to the use of judges, trained and skilled in the testing of a witness's credibility and, even more so, the witness's reliability in giving his testimony. The same approach would apply to the expert witness, testifying on technological or scientific issues.

So far as the public inquiry involves an exercise in fact-finding, the judge may sensibly be the preferred option to the unqualified chairman. Where the public inquiry involves the chairman having the task of evaluating issues outside the purview of litigation and intrudes upon the evaluation of a public issue, there are substantial issues of a more general requirement that judges in litigation often do not experience. It is entirely apt to regard the fact-finding process as a judge-like exercise. But where the public inquiry is asked to pass judgment on matters of system and services in public affairs, there are very different considerations. The best example can be taken from the diametrically opposite function of the lawyer from that of a politician or civil servant. The *Arms to Iraq* Inquiry prompts the distinction.

## The Scott Inquiry

In the Scott Inquiry, the relevant minister at the Foreign Office, Lord Waldegrave, was, predictably, unrepresented, but was provisionally criticised in a draft of the report (that was sent to him for any response he might make) for deliberately misleading Parliament about the government's policy towards the international sale of arms. The minister was thus alerted to the possible criticism, and responded to the effect that there was no misunderstanding in his statement to Parliament. The final report modified the original criticism, to the extent of exonerating the minister from any intent to misrepresent, or 'lie'. The textual modification, however, did not allay the rival arguments. The initial, unamended, criticism in Sir Richard Scott's report that the minister had 'lied' to Parliament has itself become subject, justifiably, to severe public criticism of the conclusion that the 'change' in government policy on the international trade in weaponry was a deception to Parliament of the true position. The legal language was in direct contrast to the language employed by a civil servant in ministerial letters from the Foreign Office to Parliament and the public, when that policy on the arms trade had not, in fact, changed.

The contretemps over the 'deceit' in informing Parliament was certainly more important than the language used by differing professionals. It denoted a difference in the use of language in the cultural life of a judge or a lawyer from that of an administrator in a complex department of State. An exposition of this fundamental difference has never been better stated than by Lord Wilberforce in a House of Lords debate on 7 February 1996. His speech clearly and concisely differentiated the thought-process of a trained lawyer from that of a high-ranking civil servant. He said:

> From the period that I had in the Civil Service I learnt three things: first, the enormous complexity of the nature of government in the formation and carrying out of policy, especially where several departments are concerned. It is difficult to obtain a clear, consistent, easily describable picture. The whole thing is muddy and not transparent. Secondly, I received a clear impression which I retain to this day of the remarkably high standard of integrity—and that hardly needs saying—and also of concern in the Administration for constitutional propriety, especially in relations with Parliament. There is an almost obsessive care in securing the accuracy of information supplied to Parliament. It exists and always has existed. Thirdly, I recognise a degree of tension between the Executive on the one hand and the legal system and the judiciary on the other. There is the consciousness that out there, in the legal system, are methods of thought, sets of values, and conventions which are different and which above all use a different language from the methods, conventions and language used by those who form government policy...

> It is quite clear that Sir Richard Scott, in his report, has accepted in full that Mr Waldegrave had no intention to mislead Parliament. His honour is totally cleared; it ought never to have been impugned. What is in some dispute perhaps is whether what he said or wrote about the Government's policy was objectively misleading to Parliament. The Scott Report says yes, and that we have to consider for ourselves...

> The lawyer's approach, which is basically the approach of the report, is to take the words used, compare them with a set of facts which is found to be established and then to judge whether there is a discrepancy between the two. If so, it is misleading. That is what Scott did in the report. He took the words used by Mr. Waldegrave, quoted them and said: "No possible reading of those words used could be taken to conform with the facts". That is what the noble Baroness, Lady Thatcher, described as legal "exactitude".

> However, there is another approach... It is an altogether broader approach. We must consider what was said in the context in which it was used. The context is of an accepted practice, known well to Parliament, that one does not give particulars of arms sales, especially

where two different states are concerned. I need not emphasise to your Lordships that the states concerned are Iran and Iraq, which presented a situation of particular sensitivity all through the relevant period. We must consider statements in the context of the guidelines which were confessedly and purposely made flexible. We must consider that it was obvious to everyone, as the noble and learned Lord, Lord Hailsham, made clear that Guideline 3 could not continue to apply after the ceasefire. That was self-evident and therefore there had to be some change. In the admirable words of the noble Baroness, Lady Thatcher, there was an "evolution of the guidelines", under changing circumstances. That is what existed and it was part of the context.

We must also consider that the context of what was involved was not the supply of weapons or what is called "lethal" equipment, but mainly machine tools. We must consider the context that what was relevant and important in the way of intelligence had not been made available to the Ministers concerned. All that was part of a complex system, worked out across the departments and known well to exist by Parliament, to whom the statements were made.

The system may be unsatisfactory. The very great value of the Scott Report is that it gives the arguments and the materials and it points the way for a change in approach if Parliament chooses to take it, in the direction of less secrecy or further examination by Parliament. But it would be wrong and wholly unjust to lay criticism, and still less sanctions, on those persons who, let us remember, were not centrally in the policy area and who bona fide—and I emphasise bona fide—had been working the system in what they saw to be the national interest. There is no dispute about it, in the end it was in the national interest.[3]

It all turned on the Inquiry's provisional conclusion that, in Lord Waldegrave's letters to members of the public and in his statement to Parliament, there had been no change in the guidance to arms dealers on sales of arms to Iraq and other countries. The 'warning notice' from Sir Richard Scott to Lord Waldegrave stated that the latter had lied when signing the letters. He had positively deceived those receiving the information; the guidelines had, in effect, indicated official change. Lord Waldegrave's lawyers metaphorically asked, 'What is the evidence that the guidelines had changed?', to which the administrators in government replied, comprehensively after a rummage through their files, 'there isn't any'; in which case the guidelines had *not* changed. When Sir Richard Scott was then informed of Lord Waldegrave's more complete response to the provisional criticism, the published version was that there had been a deception, but that Lord Waldegrave did not intend to deceive, and was acquitted of lying. He was, however, still criticised for his sophistry. He was, however, not mollified by the lessening of the criticism; his reputation had still been tarnished.

We should abandon the qualification of 'judicial' as a species of public inquiries, apart from the three forms of government, if only to take steps to avoid confused thinking about what we want to achieve in public inquiries. We still incline

---

[3] HL Deb, 26 February 1996, vol 569, cols 1298–1300.

(although, happily, this is fast disappearing) to the belief that keeping politics and law in separate compartments is a good thing (even, disastrously, of constitutional significance). When judges are demonstrably dubbed by Parliament in the Inquiries Act 2005, at the request of ministers of the Crown, to promote the disclosure of the truth of events of public disaster or social scandal, we should call a spade a spade: the judge is a commissioner of inquiry. The judge, unfettered by the judicial oath that binds him in ordinary litigation, steps down from the Bench, where he is rightly venerated for his independence and impartiality. *A priori*, he assists the government to amplify the trend for peace, order and good government.

# 10

## Counsel to the Inquiry, Statutory and Non-statutory

If there is only, since the Inquiries Act 2005, a very limited role in statutory public inquiries for counsel to represent the interests of witnesses to the inquiry (by the limited concept of the 'core participant'), the opposite conclusion must be drawn in respect of counsel for the inquiry. As Lord Woolf proclaimed in the House of Lords debate on 19 March 2015, on the motion to take note of the select committee's report on the Inquiries Act 2005,[1] he regarded counsel to an inquiry as 'critical'. Counsel oversees and prepares evidence, questions witnesses, advises the inquiry and essentially assists the chairman in interpreting and guiding the proceedings. He is always the confidant of his chairman, and he is there to help the secretariat. Just so, but there is little definitive about the precise role of counsel. First, it should be noted that there is no statutory obligation to appoint counsel, and there is little written about counsel's duty to the inquiry. But rarely has any inquiry dispensed with the role of counsel. Although pressed from many quarters, the Chilcot Inquiry (2009–16) declined to appoint counsel, although legal advice and assistance of distinction came from a member of the legal team that supported the acquisition and analysis of written material—a vital expedient of an inquiry's task. With or without any legal representation to the inquiry, there can only be an examination of witnesses in their oral evidence independent of the panel members. It is highly desirable that, apart from helpful intervention from panel members, any questioning should give no impression of potential assessment by the panel of the credibility or reliability of a witness's evidence. As Sir Stephen Sedley told the Committee,[2] the reason why it is wise to have counsel to an inquiry is that if the chair (or any panel member) starts asking all the questions, there is a real risk that at some point he or she is going to look *parti pris*, and there is a loss of that impartiality that the panel needs to convey throughout. The report of the select committee said this:

> Some inquiries seem to have managed without counsel. Alun Evans explained that in the Foot and Mouth Inquiry 'the chairman was absolutely adamant that he did not want

---

[1] HL Deb 19 March 2015, vol 700, cols 1141–42.
[2] para 216, p 67.

permanent access to counsel.' The Iraq Inquiry has not used counsel, but Sir John Chilcot told us: 'The absence of Counsel to the Inquiry undoubtedly placed an additional onus on myself and my colleagues in relation to the questioning of each witness who appeared before us. When preparing for our public hearings, we were assisted by staff employed within the Inquiry Secretariat and received some expert guidance on the questioning of witnesses.' Sir Stephen Sedley pointed out that the Iraq Inquiry not only had no counsel but no practising lawyer on the panel, and 'some of us reading the daily reports of what was going on were almost weeping at the questions that were not being asked.' ...

The expense of counsel to the inquiry is undoubtedly considerable, though for the reasons advanced in chapter 5 we do not think it need be inordinate. We do not know whether the Court received evidence that the cost would be 'disproportionate'. The evidence we received from Lee Hughes (whose experience, as we have said, was very substantial) was, on the contrary, that the use of counsel could save money: 'I am a great believer in having counsel to the inquiry leading and focusing the questioning of witnesses. The biggest cost in an inquiry is the length. If you can keep the inquiry shorter, you save money. There are various ways you can do that but one of them, I think, is having counsel to the inquiry taking the major responsibility for the questioning of witnesses.' We stress that, ultimately, the responsibility for the questioning will be that of the chairman.

Decision-makers should, ostensibly at the very least, retain observably their neutrality. Fairness demands no more than members reserving their decision-making, other than vocally during the hearings.

Apart from the questioning of witnesses by counsel to the Inquiry, the use by the panel of a skilled advocate inevitably discloses a close working relationship between the chairman and the panel members with counsel. It is important that the identification of eliciting and testing the reliability of evidence readily spills over to the product of decision-making. Should the drafting of the report therefore be the exclusive task of those nominated to make the decision? It is understandable that many panels rely on counsel to the inquiry to include in his duties some assistance in drafting the report. Whether or not counsel to an inquiry ceases to function at the closure of examining witnesses, there is everything to be said for the precise scope of counsel's duty being announced. The preference is for the chairman to indicate that the panel alone will draft the report, exclusive of the assistance of counsel to the inquiry. Asking pertinent questions, repeatedly, is a different role from assessing the witnesses' answers. But at the last the public should know that the task of reporting to the relevant minister is the chairman's.

# 11

## Safeguards for Witnesses

The fundamental principle of fairness to witnesses in public inquiries, which for 40 years had buttressed the Six Cardinal Principles of the Salmon Report of 1966, has not vanished from the process of a public inquiry; in fact, it has simply shifted its position to the point of reporting in the inquisitorial procedure (without, largely, any legal representation since the 2005 Act). It is now at the chairman's point of reporting to the sponsoring minister that the witness looks for a notice of any potential criticism in the final report. What has been seriously overlooked in the debate over warnings to witnesses has been the discarded procedure of Salmon letters. The fact is that the Salmon letter has now become inoperative; it was always 'sterile in legal effect'. Why should it be any more strengthened in its effect, merely because fairness functions at a later stage in the process?

As long ago as 1974, in *Maxwell v Department of Trade and Industry* (which spawned the label of 'Maxwellisation'),[1] the Court of Appeal decided, in a case involving companies legislation, that the report of an inspector of companies neither produced, nor could it directly produce, any legal consequence. As Lord Justice Lawton, in an assenting judgment, said:[2]

> On receiving it [the report] the Minister had to decide what action to take; and even if the inquiry had been conducted unfairly the report might have contained information which the Minister would be under a duty to consider for the purpose of performing his statutory duty to safeguard the interests of shareholders. The fact is that a declaration to the effect that the inquiry had been conducted unfairly or that specified criticisms had been made unfairly would produce no practical result. The Minister would not be stopped from initiating proceedings if he thought that the facts justified such a course. It was submitted that such a declaration would protect the plaintiff's reputation. It might; but the protection would only be temporary if the Minister initiated proceedings; and in any proceedings the fact that the inquiry had been conducted unfairly would be irrelevant.

And, pointedly, Lord Justice Lawton added: 'A man who has been unfairly criticised in a report made under section 165 [of the Companies Act 1948] is in the same position as one who had been unfairly criticised in a speech made in Parliament. He has suffered "damnum" but not "injuria."' A reputation may be harmed,

---

[1] *Maxwell v Department of Trade and Industry* [1974] QB 523.
[2] At p 543.

but not in any way that would be recognised in law. So it is in the case of a report of a public inquiry submitted to the minister under the Inquiries Act 2005. The chairman's report in a public inquiry is akin to a speech in Parliament.

There is another good reason for denying any legal consequence from the chairman's right to exercise his freedom of expression. Fairness in conducting the inquiry (as imposed statutorily) imposes only on the chairman and his co-panel-lists an imperfect duty. The perfection of that duty of fairness is effected (if at all) by the sponsoring minister.

# Scope of the Report

Under the Inquiries Act 2005, the ambit of the inquiry chairman's duty is to deliver the report to the minister. It must set out the facts found or determined and, where the terms of reference require it, include any recommendations. Additionally, the report may also contain anything else considered to be relevant to the terms of reference. By section 25 it is the minister's duty to arrange the publication of an inquiry's report. The minister may delegate to the chairman the arrangement for publication. The limitation on what the report is entitled to contain is provided in section 2 of the Inquiries Act 2005. The inquiry is '*not* [italics supplied] to rule on, and has no power to determine any person's civil or criminal liability'. This prohibition as to what the inquiry report may contain is suitably circumscribed by the statutory provision, that 'an inquiry is not to be inhibited by any likelihood of liability being inferred from facts that it determines or recommendations that it makes'.

Rule 13(3) of the Inquiry Rules 2006 is, more than arguably, invalid for want of statutory authority. Rule 13 imposes no *duty* on an inquiry to serve a warning letter; indeed, rule 13(1) makes it clear that the inquiry has a discretion whether as a matter of fairness to send a warning letter. But rule 13(3) says that 'the panel may not include criticism in a report to the Minister unless a warning letter has been sent to the person concerned and that person has been given a reasonable opportunity to respond to this warning letter'.[3] To complete the fasciculus of the provisions for giving the warning letter, I must add rule 15, which leaves the chairman of the inquiry no discretion with regard to the content of warning letters:

15.—(1) Subject to paragraphs (3) and (4), the warning letter must—

(a)  state what the criticism or proposed criticism is;
(b)  contain a statement of the facts that the chairman considers substantiate the criticism or proposed criticism; and
(c)  refer to any evidence which supports those facts.

---

[3] See J Beer, *Public Inquiries* (Oxford University Press, 2011) paras 9.34–9.37, p 365.

(2) The chairman may provide copies of the evidence referred to with the warning letter, if he considers it appropriate to do so.

(3) Where the warning letter is sent to a person under rule 13(1)(b)—

(a)   the requirements of paragraph (1) do not apply, but
(b)   subject to paragraph (4), the letter must refer to the evidence from which criticism could be inferred.

(4) Paragraphs (1) to (3) are subject to any restrictions on the disclosure of evidence, documents or information pursuant to sections 19 and 23 of the Act, or resulting from a determination of public interest immunity.

Two consequences flow from section 2. First, the exclusion from the report of any finding of civil or criminal liability renders the public inquiry outwith the purview of Article 6 of the European Convention on Human Rights requiring fair treatment to any person in the determination of any civil or criminal liability; there is thus an absence of any judicial power. Second, any finding of the inquiry as to blameworthiness or fault on the part of any person (which might be classified under the rubric of 'criticism') is otherwise absolutely preserved to the inquiry report. This in turn is a statutory reflection of the attitude of the common law. It finds a classic expression in the judgment of Lord (then Mr) Justice Laws in *R v Advertising Standards Authority Ltd, ex parte Vernon Organisation Ltd*. In that case, the Advertising Standards Authority (ASA) investigated and upheld a complaint that an advertisement was in breach of the British Code of Advertising Practice, which the ASA proposed to publish as its decision. Vernons, a company which specialised in promoting a football pools competition, applied to restrain the ASA from publishing its decision; the application was refused:

> ... there is a general principle in our law that the expression of opinion and the conveyance of information will not be restrained by the courts save on pressing grounds. Freedom of expression is as much a sinew of the common law as it is of the European Convention on Human Rights ...[4]

Unless there are 'pressing grounds' for limiting the scope of the inquiry's report to the minister—something akin to prior restraint on freedom of speech—the 'sending of a warning letter' in rule 13(3) of the Inquiry Rules 2006 is *ultra vires* the Inquiries Act 2005, and illegal. The essential vice is the effective prohibition on the chairman in exercising his power to criticise. Even if there may be pressing grounds for letters of warning to those who may be criticised in the inquiry report,

---

[4] *R v Advertising Standards Authority Ltd, ex p Vernon Organisation Ltd* [1992] 1 WLR 1289 at 1293A. Similarly, the power of the Metropolitan Police (under sch 7 to the Terrorism Act 2000) to stop and question a suspect of terrorism was potentially incompatible with the freedom of expression in relation to journalistic material. So too, the publication of a decision to ban an advertisement would infringe upon the freedom of expression of a commission of inquiry's report to the sponsoring minister: *R (Miranda) v Secretary of State for the Home Department* [2016] EWCA Civ 6.

it would be introducing a safeguard greater than that accorded under the Salmon letter system. Such a piece of reform would be surprising, given the nature of the administrative process since 2005.

## Fairness

The reference to 'fairness' in section 17(3) cannot sensibly be referable exclusively to an individual person, whether as a 'core participant' or other interested party. Since the wording of 'fairness' relates to 'making any decision *as to the procedure or conduct of an inquiry*' [italics supplied] by the chairman, the provision must refer to fair treatment collectively to all witnesses appearing before the inquiry and not to any individual party. It is also submitted that fairness in the procedure or conduct of the proceedings includes consideration of fairness to the public generally.

## Prior Warning of Criticism

What then remains in the aim and purpose of rule 13(3)—other than to ascertain whether it could ever be a safeguard to potential blameworthiness sufficient to contribute 'pressing grounds'? It must be assumed that Parliament, in the Inquiries Act 2005, specifically declined to enact the principle of Salmon letters.[5] Their re-emergence in a different guise in rule 13, if otherwise valid, in fact goes far beyond what Salmon letters required. It was never the practice of tribunals to require public inquiries to give notice of criticism that was contemplated in the reports to the sponsoring authority, although sometimes a party was told of an intended criticism. Any blameworthiness would be alerted to the witness before he came to give his evidence so as to avoid any allegations of criticism.

# What Constitutes 'Pressing Grounds'?

It is interesting to note an observation of Mr Justice Laws in the *ASA* case. He noted (at p 1293G) that there was no reason why a public body's duty to express an opinion (such as a public inquiry under the Inquiries Act 2005) should be subject to any less rigid rules than a private individual. If anything, he added, the case is analogous to one where an administrative body has an adjudicative function

---

[5] The Salmon Six Principles, although strictly abolished in 2005, may appear to survive judicially in a limited form in the independent territories: see the decision of the Judicial Committee of the Privy Council in *R, ex p Mario Hoffman v The Commissioner of Inquiry and the Governor of the Turks and Caicos* [2012] UKPC 17, para 38.

and in the course of its public duties publishes a ruling criticising some affected person, and the ruling is later disturbed or reversed by an appropriate appellate body. An inquiry under the Inquiries Act 2005 is an 'administrative body'. If those to be criticised should have some safeguard against publication, any warning letter should come from the minister as publisher.

What may constitute 'pressing grounds'? In paragraph 247 of the report of the House of Lords Select Committee, Sir Brian Leveson (who conducted the 2010–11 inquiry into the culture, practices and ethics of the British press) told the Committee that if he had followed the Rules 'to the letter', he would never have finished his inquiry. (His counsel, Robert Jay QC—now Mr Justice Jay—spoke in a similar vein; he was also condemning of the supposed removal of the chairman's discretion to provide the witness with an absolute safeguard.) Sir Brian appears to have sensibly avoided the requirement under the Rules, to give notice if criticism was intended. Sir Brian might have aired the dilemma by taking note of a submission I made to him in writing, arguing that the Rules were *ultra vires*. If he had found that rules 13–15 were illegal and needed revision, it might by now have prompted the desired reform.

It is interesting to note the conclusion of the Ministry of Justice's *Memorandum to the Justice Select Committee: Post-Legislative Assessment of the Inquiries Act 2005* in October 2010. It stated:

> We have no evidence of any serious suggestion that the Act should be repealed in any substantive way. The overwhelming evidence, however, is that the Inquiry Rules [2006] as currently drafted are unduly restrictive and do not always enable the most effective operation of the Act.[6]

# Fairness in Reporting

When the Select Committee of the House of Lords reported in March 2014 on the early functioning of the Inquiries Act 2005, it welcomed the replacement of the 1921 Act with a uniform model for public inquiries; it specifically was out of favour with the Inquiry Rules 2006 made as delegated legislation in its provisions for the writing of the individual chairman's report to the sponsoring minister. And a year later, on 19 March 2015, in a debate in the House of Lords on a motion to take note of the select committee's report,[7] all the speakers who mentioned the Rules (apart from the minister) were critical of them. While there was a good intent to provide a full and suitable basis for future inquiries, it urged a speedy repeal of the Rules. A signal was given on the current regulations [rule 13 of the Inquiry Rules

---

[6] Cm 7943, para 70.
[7] HL Deb 19 March 2015, vol 760, cols 1134–79.

2006] by Lord Pannick QC; he said that they 'must go'.[8] What, if anything, should replace the regulations about the chairman's writing of the report? Lord Pannick's answer was short and swift. He asserted that if in a court of law it was not right for a witness to be shown a draft of the judgment (i.e. where there is no disclosure before judgment is delivered), 'it is all the more so when we are talking about the report of an inquiry'—which is not a tribunal or a court of law. A judgment of a court is, however, dissimilar to the inquiry report. Once a fair hearing is concluded in the courts, nobody is entitled to a sight of the court's judgment upon which the witness could be asked to comment on any implied or express criticism before the report is finalised. If the public inquiry is *not* a species of litigation, but is an aspect of public administration, how can the same principle apply? I think it cannot, if only because the report is an offshoot of government through its departments of State, and carries no weight of legal enforcement, save at most a recommendation to the sponsoring minister. It proclaims a public verdict; it gives no judgment that demands enforcement by order of the legal system. But, as much as the chairman thinks fit, the principle of flexibility leaves a decision to warn the witness of some blameworthiness, and sometimes prompts fairness in providing an opportunity for a re-think or a comment on a matter not satisfactorily dealt with in the course of the inquiry. There may be a failure to disclose a vital document; exceptionally, a witness may expect to be given a warning if a crucial issue has not hitherto come to light. This situation is thus strikingly different from litigation between rival disputants who are in total command of determining the adducing of evidence to the court. Witnesses at a public inquiry are devoid of any entitlement to selection of testimony; they are called (or not) at the behest of the public inquiry before whom they are unrepresented, unless they qualify under a strictly limited right to address the inquiry as 'core participants', and then only on matters unconnected with the accumulation of oral evidence.

The drafting of rule 13 establishing the duty to issue a warning notice to a witness who is provisionally identified as blameworthy is all the more astonishing in the light of the existing jurisprudence on administrative tribunals. When Robert Maxwell was subject to disciplinary proceedings that made him susceptible to disqualification from company directorship, he sought to be alerted in advance of the report on his dealings before Mr Owen Stable QC issued his published findings. He claimed that it was only fair that he should be able to comment upon anticipated criticism of his directorship. He failed, on the ground that there was no legal obligation on the inquirer under the Companies Act to warn him of potential criticism. For 40 years, no one doubted the Maxwellisation doctrine.

No doubt the disciplinary proceeding over the management of a public company was treated as an aspect of public law and decidedly not a finding of civil or criminal liability equivalent to a judgment of a court of law. The proceedings

---

[8] HL Deb 19 March 2015, vol 760, cols 1152–53.

under the companies legislation were like those of a public inquiry; the surveillance of companies by the Registrar of Companies is a part of public administration and public law. There remains a discretion to alert a witness to fend off a publishable criticism. The select committee so recommended: it stated:

> We recommend that rules 13–15 of the Inquiry Rules 2006 should be revoked and a rule to the following effect substituted: 'If the chairman is considering including in the report significant criticism of a person, and he believes that that person should have an opportunity to make a submission or further submission, he should send that person a warning letter and give him a reasonable opportunity to respond.'[9]

In spite of all the criticism in the debate in the House of Lords on 19 March 2015—at least those lawyerly Lords suggested that rules 13–15 must go—the Minister, Lord Faulks (since the election in May 2015 still the same office-holder), said as follows:

> I now come to what is much more controversial: the question why Her Majesty's Government rejected the Committee's recommendation that Rules 13 to 15 on warning letters should be revoked and substituted with the rule giving chairs greater discretion.

The rest of the government's response (as at April 2016) is stubborn silence. As Lord Brown of Eaton-under-Heywood (himself a distinguished retired Law Lord) said:

> In short, the Government's bland rejection of this recommendation is surely to be regarded as deeply unsatisfactory and indeed somewhat disingenuous. Nothing could be more obviously calculated to result in future inquiries suffering the same problems of delay and expense. I say 'needlessly' because the rule proposed to substitute for Rules 13 to 15 would provide precisely the flexibility to enable chairmen in future to ensure fairness in the particular circumstances of each case. The recommendation makes obvious good sense and should be accepted and implemented without further delay.

## The Chilcot Inquiry

But delay there has been, as evidenced by the worry over the report of the Chilcot Inquiry. A parliamentary committee considering the HBOS affair has appointed Mr Andrew Green QC and his barristerial colleagues to review the process that many people blame for the inordinate delay in the release of Sir John Chilcot's report into the Iraq war of 2001. Although Sir John made it clear

---

[9] para 251, p 76. It endorsed the conclusion by the Ministry of Justice in its memorandum in October 2010 to the Justice Select Committee in its post-legislative assessment of the Inquiries Act 2005 that 'the overwhelming evidence … is that the Inquiry Rules as currently drafted are unduly restrictive and do not always enable the most effective operation of the Act'.

from the outset in the inquiry, ordered in 2009 by Gordon Brown as Prime Minister, that potential witnesses would be given the opportunity to comment on any criticism in the pending report, it was not a warning notice under the Inquiry Rules 2006, or indeed under the Act of 2005 itself. It was made, pointedly, under prerogative powers that reflect its political significance. Sir John appears to have adopted the 'normal practice' in the Inquiries Act 2005 that the witness should be warned of any potential criticism—known as Maxwellisation—and whether such a promise should automatically be made in future inquiries, as it exists in rules 13–15 of the Inquiry Rules 2006. In the present state of uncertainty, Andrew Bailey and Brian Pomeroy, who are leading the inquiry into the near-demise of HBOS, have said that Maxwellisation is 'legally required'. But is Maxwellisation just a matter of custom and not obligatory? The question, hugely controversial, remains unanswered as yet.

## The Conduct of the Inquiry

Assuming that Sir John Chilcot and his fellow panellists were embarked upon a novel avenue of inquiry, as a result of the responses from witnesses who received warning letters of potential criticisms, the question arises as to the terms of reference. Presumably, these responses stem from documentary material previously undisclosed; if so, what prevented the completeness of the inquiry during the first two years of gathering evidence in 2009–11. But it may involve only the interpretation of uncovered evidence, which is questionable or arguably wrong, and may need to be verified afresh.

That issue apart, the question is posed whether the mode of inquiry was deficient in the scope of the inquiry. From the outset, Sir John was keen to de-legalise the process; no legal representation for witnesses (or core participants) was countenanced. Indeed, initially it was decreed that the inquiry would be held in private; subsequently the examination of witnesses was conducted openly, and televised. The decision to exclude legal representation was complemented by an absence (other than as part of the inquiry's team analysing the documentary material) of the traditional practice of nominating counsel to the inquiry, as advisors to the chairman, or, more directly, for the examination of the witnesses. I can personally testify that Sir John was pressed to follow the practice. He declined, on the ground that the process was to be conducted extra-legally, and that the panellists were capable of interrogating the witnesses to the inquiry's satisfaction; it also constituted a public message that the examination of witnesses was to be exploratory and not confrontational. Advocacy skills were to be avoided, not just to save time and costs, but also to incline towards investigation rather than resolve dispute about personal liability for the war on Iraq.

In the perceived circumstances, questioning of witnesses was distinctly not lawyerly; it noticeably lacked the incisiveness of professionally skilled advocates. Questions tended, with some rare exceptions, to be amiable, non-contentious and lacking the expected skills of a distinguished Queen's Counsel. Comparison was contemporaneously made with the role of counsel to the Leveson Inquiry during 2011. The conclusion has been drawn that the area of controversial decision-making about 'going to war' was a lost opportunity. Does the nature of the process determine the question of warning witnesses of criticism for them to refute or amend?

The Inquiries Act 2005 expressly preserves 'any power of Her Majesty to establish a Royal Commission', and 'any power of a Minister … to cause an inquiry to be held otherwise than under the Act'.[10] Thus the distinction between the statutory form of inquiry and the non-statutory exception. The Chilcot Inquiry was under the exceptional form of inquiry; it is somewhat surprising therefore that it should describe its witnesses' access to 'relevant sections of the draft report in order to make any representations on the proposed criticism prior to publication of the final report'.[11]

The distinction relates to the subject matter which causes public concern and does not discriminate as between witnesses to the event under reference. Significantly, however, the inquiry calls for two determinations—fact-finding decisions and their impact upon political systems and services. They demand different methods of inquiry, the latter focusing on opinions and value-judgments. It may be that the extra-statutory inquiries rely more heavily on given data on which human testimony is more easily assessed. The statutory injunction to steer clear of legal liability further indicates a rejection of the litigious process and aims at issues beyond blame. Systems and services provide the essential background to individual action.

Since the duty of the reporters of inquiries is imperfect, in that they are sterile of legal effect, there can be nothing to infer a right to an opportunity to forestall criticism. A damage to one's reputation, as Lord Justice Lawton aptly stated in the Maxwell case, is wounding, but it does not cause any physical harm. Nor should it, when the inquiry is extra-statutory. Fairness to witnesses in referred events is likewise treated in the realm of information, true or false. It functions legally only in the qualified form of tortious libel, as in the advertisement case.

---

[10] s 44.
[11] Protocol for witnesses giving evidence to the Iraq Inquiry, s 30.

# 12

## Chilcot-Maxwellisation-Saville: The Problem of Delay

The procedure for safeguarding the interests of witnesses in the Chilcot Inquiry was uniquely an amalgam of two attitudes to the proceedings of public inquiries. From the outset, Sir John Chilcot disavowed any participation in the hearings by the legal representatives of potential witnesses; in so doing he adopted the techniques of Sir Richard Scott in the *Arms to Iraq* Inquiry of 1993–96, but at the same time, by the issuance of a witness protocol, warned witnesses in advance of their evidence of any potential criticisms and indicated that they would have the opportunity to meet any criticism in the draft of his report. Hence, a potential delay in publicising the report (which turned out to be almost two years, from October 2014 to July 2016) was always contemplated (and effectively telegraphed).

The Chilcot Inquiry established initially a witness protocol[1] which outlined to all potential witnesses the aims and purposes of the Inquiry, and additionally promised any witness notice of impending criticism in the final report, so that such a witness would have the opportunity to respond to the criticism, given the relevant passage in the report. The warning of potential criticism had never been sanctioned in earlier, traditional reports; they focused on the jurisprudence, known as Maxwellisation, which did not signal any harm to the witness's reputation. The warning contemplated roughly what was envisaged in rules 13–15 of the Inquiry Rules 2006.

The inevitable delay in reporting, in terms of time and cost, by the approach of alerting the witness in advance, was the subject of instantaneous adverse comment by Lord Saville, in an article for *The Brief*, an online legal magazine.

Whatever may be the correct view (until the late 1990s) of warning witnesses to a public inquiry of the impending blameworthiness of their actions (or inactions), I find the attitude of Lord Saville perplexing. In his criticism of Sir John Chilcot, Lord Saville made no reference to the Inquiry Rules 2006 which supplemented the Inquiries Act 2005 in abolishing the 1921 Act, and which effectively abandoned the procedure operative from 1966 onwards. Moreover, the discarding of the Six

---

[1] Annex 3 below.

Cardinal Principles from the Salmon report, which were excoriatingly damned by Sir Richard Scott in his report on the Arms to Iraq inquiry in 1996, was disconcertingly overlooked by Lord Saville, both in the Bloody Sunday Inquiry and in the attack on Sir John Chilcot. But that is not all. The House of Lords select committee on the function of the Inquiries Act, in March 2014, had endorsed the 2005 Act (with a major qualification of the rule establishing the warning notice in the draft report of impending criticism); that endorsement was confirmed by the House of Lords itself in March 2015.

Sir John Chilcot had been poised in October 2014 to deliver publicly his report, set up by the then Prime Minister, Gordon Brown, in 2009; the 2.6 million words of the Inquiry report appeared on 6 July 2016, at an estimated cost of £10 million. The reason for delaying the publication had been contemplated well in advance. On the face of it, fairness (inserted specifically by Parliament in section 17(3) of the 2005 Act) provided the various witnesses with an opportunity to respond to criticism in the draft report, as well as having received copies of the evidence given just after they had provided oral testimony in open session to the panellists. The delay is explicable because it impliedly followed the judgments of the Court of Appeal in the *Maxwell* case, which at the time (1974) did not impart any legal remedy, even if it appeared to be unfair to the witness during the inquiry. The law provided that if there had been any unfairness in the inquiry, so be it. The recommendation in the House of Lords debate in March 2015 on the Inquiries Act 2005 of flexibility in warning witnesses prior to full publication was not unconditional. The inquiry chairman was fully entitled *not* to give any warning to a criticised witness. The witness's appearance, on being warned of the scope of his evidence, was like any recipient of an official complaint in a public forum. As Lord Justice Lawton said in the *Maxwell* case, criticism in a public inquiry was like a speech in Parliament; there was no need to issue a warning of impending criticism. Doubtless, criticism might be damaging to the witness's reputation. But it would cause no damage which would lead to a remedial award from the court.

If the statute of 2005 demands the duty of fairness (as it clearly does), that is the moment to issue a warning—a distinct opportunity to respond effectively to the implied criticism. It was exactly the position of Robert Maxwell when he appeared in 1974 before the company inspector appointed under the companies legislation. Thereafter, he could not complain if the inspector deduced that the witness had had the opportunity to ward off any criticism. Fairness during the proceedings to anyone interested in the public inquiry may demand a forewarning, but not a specific notice to an individual at the stage of concluding the inquiry. Without the role of counsel to the inquiry effectively covering the relevant evidence during the witness's testimony, there is not, I think, fair treatment; the witness will have insufficient warning of impending criticism unless at the stage of reporting (and further delay in supplying the draft of the impending criticism) it is provided. It is crucial to ensure that the witness's evidence is probed, for a proper assessment to be made. Anything less than examination of a witness leaves open the question whether it suffices as sound evaluation, for subsequent observation. The absence of counsel to the inquiry in the Chilcot Inquiry was noticeable, in that the questioning by the panellists and decision-maker was gentle and generally lacked incisiveness.

On the publication on 6 July 2016 of the Chilcot Inquiry, Lord Saville criticised Sir John Chilcot and his colleagues for giving some witnesses the opportunity to comment on impending criticisms. Lord Saville said that there was 'no *legal* basis for providing [those criticised] with any further opportunity to comment' on the findings of the report.[2] Lord Saville's immediate outburst is breathtaking, if not positively impudent. His attitude confirms his legalistic procedure; at the same time it misunderstands the main purpose of a public inquiry. Sir John Chilcot justifiably followed the procedure unanimously recommended in March 2014 by the select committee of the House of Lords on the workings of the 2005 Act, whereby there is at least a discretion given to the inquiry to provide an opportunity to respond to potential criticism. Chilcot states that that is the purpose, often misleadingly referred to as 'Maxwellisation'. Witnesses had given evidence in accordance with the terms of paragraph 10 of the witness protocol, which provides:

> 10. The prime purpose of the Inquiry is to identify lessons to be learned. The inquiry is not a court of law and nobody will be on trial, although the committee will not shy away from making criticisms if warranted. In the event that a particular witness may be the subject of criticism by the Inquiry, the Inquiry Secretariat will, in accordance with normal practice, notify that witness separately, in writing at least seven days in advance of the evidence session, of the nature of the potential criticism and the evidence that supports it.[3]

Lord Saville's criticism of Sir John Chilcot was inept, if not inapt. To follow the procedure of a court of law (and never give prior notice) was to indulge in legalism. The witnesses were questioned not by experienced counsel, but inexpertly by the panellists. If questioning is headed by the panellists, it somewhat minimises any complaint. A witness who may have to defend his reputation should meet any criticism head-on. In Chilcot's case there was a lack of firm cross-examination.

There is a possible solution to the conundrum of supplying (or not) an opportunity to be given notice of the impending criticism. It is to leave the issue of a warning of potential criticism to the sponsor of the inquiry. Since the law under the Inquiries Act 2005 provides that it is the minister who publishes the report—although he may, of course, delegate the function—it is at that point that blameworthiness may be tested. There is a precedent for that. I experienced it when submitting the report in 1992 on allegations of ill-treatment at Ashworth Hospital. The report sent to Virginia Bottomley (the Secretary of State for Health at the time) contained a criticism of a civil servant in respect of disciplinary action against a member of the hospital staff—an individual only marginally involved in the course of the inquiry. The minister contacted me, inquiring whether the

---

[2] Italics supplied.
[3] See para 111 of the Inquiry Report, vol 1.

panel of members wished to include the specific criticism. The draft criticism was ultimately removed; the report was published, without any appreciable delay. Had the criticism been maintained, it is problematical whether the minister could have exercised her power by deleting it. Probably, yes. It might be argued that any ministerial action to meddle with specific criticism may be publicly unacceptable, since it would impinge on impartiality. But since the sponsoring minister may decide on publication, that must include undesirable items within the report.

The delay in publishing the Chilcot Report (lengthy, but not inordinate, having regard to the scope of the inquiry) was understandable. It involved giving notice to witnesses and did nothing to mar a mammoth document of 2.6 million words, a masterpiece of sound understatement, in the best British style, and lacking hyperbole. The writing was nevertheless spare and to the point in its sober narrative of an unnecessary, doubtfully illegal, war and a serious failure by the invaders to prepare for post-war reinstatement. It cost £10 million (not 200) and altogether took six years (not $12\frac{1}{2}$) to complete a vastly more complex matter—not just a tragic shooting on a single day.

# 13

## Model Inquiries: Hillsborough (1989) and Litvinenko (2015)

The terms of reference for the report in August 1989 of the public inquiry by Lord Justice Taylor (later to become Lord Chief Justice) 'into the events at Sheffield Wednesday [football stadium] on 15 April 1989, and to make recommendations about the needs of crowd control and safety at sporting events' were a model in concise and precise language. They did not seek an answer to the overriding question, why did the disaster happen. Time was short before the start of the next season of football competition, such that the main cause for the discoverable events had been overcrowding on the terraces and the fatality of 96 victims among the Liverpool fans. Significantly, however, the Inquiry declared that the disaster was caused by the failure of police control; it added, gratuitously, that 'little or no blame' was attached to the Liverpool fans; therein lay the seeds of dissension and 27 years of public action to refute the charge of blameworthiness.

The Home Secretary, in a memorandum to the Prime Minister in August 1989, observed that the most severe criticism was directed at the South Yorkshire Police: 'the main reason for the disaster was the failure of police control'. The actions of individual senior officers, especially Chief Superintendent Duckenfield, the officer in charge of the crowd at the football match, are criticised. Douglas Hurd, in his note to the Prime Minister, Margaret Thatcher, added that the Chief Constable, Peter Wright, would have to resign. His proposal was for the government to welcome the report, since the broad thrust of its theme was the devastating criticism of the police. Alternatively, it was suggested that the Home Secretary would publish the report and, without holding a press conference himself, simply issue a statement with the terms of the report. The Prime Minister, in a handwritten note, opted for the bald statement. She added: 'What do we mean by "welcoming the broad thrust of the report"?', supplying the rhetorical answer, 'the broad thrust is devastating criticism of the police; is that for us to welcome? Surely we welcome the thoroughness of the report and its recommendations.' Thus the public concern to know why the disaster that happened at the football ground was silenced for 27 years, after which the truth about the Hillsborough disaster was spelt out. The 96 Liverpool fans were unlawfully killed.

# Delayed Justice

If there is one maxim of the law that merits the 800th anniversary of Magna Carta, it is the distinct principle that emerged from the two Bloody Sunday Inquiries and the Hillsborough inquest hearings from April 2014 to April 2016, that 'justice delayed is justice denied'. Are the families of the 13 victims who were unlawfully killed by a company of paratroopers on the streets of Northern Ireland on 30 January 1972, and the families of the 96 victims at the semi-final of the FA Cup in Sheffield between Liverpool and Nottingham Forest, able to say that they have ultimately achieved justice? What they suffered, of course, was to undergo the protracted pain of grief, unrelieved by the timely verdict of unlawful killings. Grief may never vanish, but it can be officially acknowledged whenever the death is caused by the State. Does one call that justice? If so, it has certainly been long delayed for the victims and their families.

# The Litvinenko Inquiry

The report by Sir Robert Owen (a retired High Court judge), which unfolds the detailed, and remarkable, circumstances leading up to and surrounding the deliberate killing of Alexander Litvinenko in a London hotel in November 2006, reads like a detective novel.[1] In large measure, that is the result of deft handling by Sir Robert of the evidence between March and September 2015 and his exhaustive (if not exhausting) report of 21 January 2016. But the report is, horrifyingly, not fiction. It exposes the poisoning by radioactive polonium-210 poured in a pot of green tea, and sipped by Litvinenko, tracing the trail of the deposited poison by testing contamination of it at various points from Moscow to London. It identified its existence on the three actors (two killers and the victim) at hotels where they lodged and met. Sir Robert's report faithfully respects the terms of reference 'so long as the report is consistent with the ban on any finding or determination of criminal or civil liability', except by inference permissibly drawn from the inquiry's findings of fact. Adherence by Sir Robert to the restraint on any finding of liability in the case enhances the solution of the government's duty to hold a coroner's inquest into a suspicious case of a person's death, in conjunction with the human rights duty to investigate any person's death while in the custody of the State. It indicates how the two duties can be simply carried out in a public inquiry under the Inquiries Act 2005.

---

[1] The story is graphically told in L Harding *A Very Expensive Poison* (Faber Guardian, 2016).

The history of convening an inquest on the death of Alexander Livinenko was initially covered by Sir Robert as an Assistant Coroner for Inner North London. He suspended that inquest, setting out the chronology of events, and ending up with his strong recommendation that a public inquiry should instead be set up statutorily. As he records in his report,[2] 'The advantage of a public inquiry over the inquest was that the rules governing an inquiry allow for sensitive evidence to be heard in closed session'. The Home Secretary, just as promptly, declined the invitation for a full inquiry. In a letter of 7 July 2013, her reasons not to convert the inquest into a statutory inquiry were that it would take an inordinate amount of time and be costly to public funds. This was overturned by the High Court, whose reasoning was comprehensive; the judges found that the Home Secretary had 'for the time being' failed to provide a rational basis for declining to set up an inquiry under the Inquiries Act 2005.[3] Persistent advocating by Litvinenko's widow, Marina, finally induced the Home Secretary to order the merged procedure under the Inquiries Act 2005 (the widow was given 'core participant' status, as a legally represented witness, in the hearings).

Quite apart from the obligation of the state to establish a public inquiry under its obligation in Article 2 of the European Convention on Human Rights (where the death occurs in a State institution) there is no domestic law obligation to hold an independent public inquiry.[4] The Litvinenko case did not answer the question of the killer's identity and legal liability, since both of the two Russians identified as possible assassins of the émigré from Russia declined to be forensically examined as the likely perpetrators, even by video link. Other than where there is no proof of legal liability for any death, an inquiry can, as Sir Robert did, strictly adhere to its terms of reference. The way is open to combine the duties in a public inquiry under the Inquiries Act 2005.

The inquiry was set up on 31 July 2014; at that time Mr Justice Owen was a serving judge; he retired from that position in September 2014.[5] The merged proceedings began in March 2015, and Sir Robert took only six months to complete a report on his findings, which depended on outstanding detective work, tracing the destiny of the handling of the poison from Russia to Spain, Germany, and ultimately placed in a teapot at the Millennium Hotel, London.

---

[2] para 2.7 on p 9.
[3] *R v Secretary of State for the Home Department* [2014] EHWC 194 (Admin). Lord Justice Richards, in not mandating any particular outcome to the critical judgment by the Secretary of State, concluded that 'it will be necessary for the Secretary of State to give fresh consideration to the exercise of her discretion'. This she did.
[4] *R (Persey) v Secretary of State for Environment, Food and Rural Affairs* [2002] EHWC 371 (Admin), [2003] QB 794.
[5] para 2.9 on p 9.

*Hillsborough and Litvinenko*

## The Construction of Section 2(1) and (2)

On this issue Sir Robert is, understandably, less than helpful. He has written[6] that 'it was difficult to deal in the abstract with the interplay between these two sections [2(1) and 2(2)] and [he] made no formal ruling on the issue'. Just so. Sir Robert is absolved from declining to expatiate on a practical statutory expression in the précis by the interplay or construction of the sections, since Sir Robert had concluded that in the instant case he was in fact identifying primarily the conduct of individuals who did not appear as witnesses in front of the tribunal, and hence did not qualify as witnesses who might potentially claim to require warning, in advance of the publication of the report, of a potential criticism or finding of blameworthiness. Sir Robert said[7] that he was 'sure' that Mr Lugovoy and Mr Kovtun had been acting on behalf of others when they poisoned Mr Litvinenko—they were the assassins—and that it was 'probable' that Mr Lugovoy had killed Mr Litvinenko by the use of the isotope polonium-210 with the assistance of Mr Kovtun. Both Russian intelligence officers were 'under the direction of the FSB [the successor to the KGB]. I would add that I regard that as a strong probability'. For good measure, Sir Robert added that the FSB operation was 'probably approved by Mr Patrushev [the head of the FSB] and [tellingly] also by President Putin'.

Nevertheless, other appropriate witnesses who were entitled to the safeguards provided in rule 13 of the Inquiry Rules 2006 did receive warning letters, but Sir Robert did not propose to publish the contents of those letters.[8] Since there appears to be no point of criticism of any other witnesses in the Inquiry, there is nothing to assist the critics (or indeed the defenders) of blameworthiness in the investigation of Mr Litvinenko's unnatural death that prompted the original demand for an inquest. But the absence of widespread criticism of rule 13, and the parliamentary request for early review, is at least underlined by the Litvinenko Inquiry. It is further support for the recommendation of the House of Lords select committee that rules 13–15 of the Inquiry Rules 2006 should be repealed.[9]

## Standards of Proof

The introduction in the report of the standards of proof used in the legal system is misguided and harks back to the legalism of earlier public inquiries. I much prefer the less specific notion of confidence or rectitude in the assessment of credibility and reliability which Lord Saville (although it was not a statutory requirement) employed in the Bloody Sunday Inquiry.[10] Given his status as the controller of the

---

[6] At p 262.
[7] At 10.14–10.16, p 246.
[8] app 1, paras 107–08, p 260.
[9] See Chapter 11 above.
[10] Lord Saville's ruling of 11 October 2004 on the standard of proof for inquiries can be found at Volume X, p298 of his report.

intelligence service, it might have been better if Sir Robert's comment on President Putin had been that it could be stated objectively that his position made one 'highly suspicious' of his knowledge or approval of the assassination. The use of the words 'probably approved' is itself ambiguous: was the knowledge before or after the assassination? But perhaps the more emphatic use of probability stems from evidence given in closed session. (It was inevitable that Sir Robert employed the language of the law courts.) At section 2.19,[11] Sir Robert states: 'The findings are clear. I am entirely confident in making them'. After this,[12] he says that

> in making findings of fact I have adopted the flexible and variable approach ... I add that where in this Report I state that 'I am sure' I will have found a fact to the criminal standard. When I use such expressions as 'I feel' or 'I am satisfied' the standard of proof will have been the ordinary civil standard of proof, namely the balance of probabilities.

Sir Robert is mildly inconsistent with these comments, apropos of the approach taken by the criminal courts to the right to silence. It is hardly sensible to adopt criminal justice principles for one purpose and to reject them for others. Either a tribunal under the Inquiries Act 2005 is a manifestation of administrative law procedures, or it imitates the fairness of criminal and civil liability. It cannot rationally be a bit of both. These methods of evidential assessment are seen in their context of a court of law, and not considered piecemeal. It all depends on the scope and function, since 2005, of a statutory inquiry. Conceptually, what is the nature of the institution in question? The Litvinenko Report makes no attempt at the philosophy of the Inquiries Act 2005; it might usefully have expounded on the rationale of public inquiries.

## Costs

There is no mention of the costs of the Litvinenko Inquiry. It was 'completed substantially within the budget prepared by the secretariat',[13] although there is no allusion to applications for funding, except that which can be made available to allow certain persons having a connection to the inquiry to receive legal representation. Some applications were made by a number of other witnesses for their expenses and legal costs. Nor is there any mention of the funding of core participants. It would be helpful in the future if a budget under the 2005 Act could be announced from the outset. It can always be updated.

The Inquiry hearing lasted for a total of 34 days; evidence was taken on 30 days. Sixty-two witnesses gave oral evidence, five of them from overseas by video link. Others gave written testimony. Given the length of the investigation, including the

---

[11] p 10.
[12] At para 2.20, p 10, referring to paras 122–23 on p 262.
[13] para 1.3 on p 7.

coroners' proceedings, the delay of four years for the conclusion of a single, but unique, death was not inordinate. Cost-wise, and delay-wise, the case is unique; its charge to public funding is incomparable. The uncovering of the 'polonium trail' by the Metropolitan Police was an example of effective forensic detective work and scientific expertise. It was justifiably applauded.

Sir Robert is disinclined to lay down the proper attitude by the chairman of a public inquiry (which is not a part of the law) to the evidence of witnesses who refuse to participate in the oral hearings. He stated.

> I ... heard submissions on the question of whether I should or should not draw adverse inferences from the silence of any individual concerned in the events which the Inquiry was investigating, or their refusal to participate, and in particular the silence or refusal of Mr Lugovoy, Mr Kovtun or authorities of the Russian State. There was a consensus that there was no need or basis for adopting the approach taken in the criminal courts to such silence. I took the view that a failure to participate or to give evidence has the obvious consequence that I would make findings of fact without the benefit or otherwise of such a contribution.[14]

> I should make it clear that I do not regard the simple fact that Mr Lugovoy and Mr Kovtun did not give evidence before me as evidence that in itself supports the proposition that they poisoned Mr Litvinenko. There was some debate about this matter, but in the end all core participants agreed that I should not draw any adverse inferences from the fact that neither man has given evidence before me (see Appendix 1, paragraph 123). I do not do so.[15]

Surely, it is time for the refusal of witnesses to assist the process of public administration of an event of public concern to carry some sanction. Should there not be at least a convention that an unreasonable refusal to participate involves intrinsically the *presumption* in a public inquiry (which is sterile of legal effect) of a finding of no credibility, or at least unreliability being attached to evidence adduced through documentary material? There is no right to force anyone to prove his or her case; in the public inquiry, however, the public is entitled to expect a helping hand from the witness giving evidence, orally as well as by written statements that are forensically untested, unless there is a good reason for not cooperating with the inquiry.

---

[14]  para 123, p 262.
[15]  para 8.83, p 194.

# Part V

# Final Thoughts

# 14

## Conclusion

The burden of this book has been to demonstrate two major changes in the practice that was ultimately confirmed in the Inquiries Act 2005. First, is the establishment statutorily of a commission of inquiry that determines how and why the event concerned happened; and does not duplicate the finding of culpability of any individual which is the remit of the established courts of law. Second, the 2005 Act adopted the changed practice of investigation without any right of the witness to be alerted to potential criticism before giving evidence, and instead safeguarding the interests of witnesses by eliciting their response to any criticism that might appear in the draft report before its publication. The book describes how the public inquiry system, since the 1966 Royal Commission, had endorsed the system adopted by lawyers representing their clients, until the procedure (particularly the need to issue 'Salmon letters', indicating allegations of blame, to witnesses) was heavily criticised by Sir Richard Scott in the *Arms to Iraq* Inquiry in 1996.

Despite the clear message from Sir Richard Scott, Lord Saville, when appointed to chair the second inquiry into the tragic events on Bloody Sunday, 30 January 1972, chose to conduct the inquiry according to the Six Cardinal Principles propounded by the 1966 Salmon Commission, with the inevitable legalism that stemmed from that decision. There was a total misunderstanding about what was required by the terms of reference given by the Secretary of State for Northern Ireland (almost a replica of the terms of reference to Lord Widgery in 1972). Put bluntly, Lord Saville's judge-like approach was intellectually flawed about what was required of the panellists, collectively (not individually), in the Bloody Sunday inquiry. Lord Saville, by his personal approach (commendably, it is conceded), was determined to undergo a 'thorough' investigation; no one should accuse the inquiry of anything less than thoroughness. The trouble was that the task was limited to identifying what happened, and why it happened. Individual blameworthiness was only an ancillary question, if at all. Lord Saville adhered, limpet-like, to the established practice that had been followed until the *Arms to Iraq* Inquiry in 1993–96. A departure in that inquiry excoriated the Six Cardinal Principles of the Salmon Commission as being inappropriate to a public inquiry that, correctly, conferred no rights (at least, no rights enforceable in any legal sense) on witnesses, and, importantly, on legal representatives who displayed their talents on behalf of clients with the aim of averting any criticism of their clients' conduct in the events under inquiry. Without examination, including the legally valuable arm of cross-examination, it would have been possible to forge ahead with the inquiry with due expedition and at a vastly reduced cost to the public purse.

A mural on the city walls of Derry, depicting Bishop Edward Daly (who died on 8 August 2016 at the age of 82) waving a bloodied white handkerchief while caring for a dying teenager under gunfire from the paratroopers of the British Army, vividly commemorates the deaths of 13 civil rights marchers in the course of the protracted Troubles in the Province. The responsibility for their deaths was officially acknowledged, commendably and unambiguously, by the Prime Minister in a statement in the House of Commons on 10 June 2010. The hurt caused by Lord Widgery's verdict in his report of April 1972 claiming the paratroopers' innocence has been refuted, and suitably buried by the inquiry by Lord Saville and his fellow panellists. Their findings fully endorsed the culpability for the deaths to the unjustified shootings by the company of paratroopers in pursuance of an 'arrest operation'. The blameworthiness of the British Army for the tragic event on 30 January 1972 was palpable.

There can be little doubt that, even among the many people who constantly wailed at the protracted delay in the publication of the report on the Bloody Sunday Inquiry, the exoneration of the victims on a civil rights march was ultimately acknowledged with profound relief. Those grieving members of the families of the 13 victims of the shots fired by the company of paratroopers had had to wait 38 years for the vindication of the victims and the thousands who survived the civil rights march. Their long wait, appropriately campaigned, was amply justified by Lord Saville and his panellists, even if the same result of the vindication of the marchers could have been reached under a much shorter, even truncated, procedure. It was not unreasonable to predict, in 1998, that the inquiry should take no more than 18 months to two years to complete the given task. But the need for expedition and reasonable cost called for explanation. Lord Saville did not apologise for the delay; the 'thoroughness' of his judicial approach made the inquiry, he asserted, inevitably lengthy.

But that was not the only factor that dictated a swifter procedure for the assigned task. Bloody Sunday was unique among inquiries. Every Tom, Dick and Harry from the media had descended on the scene of the tragedy. They accumulated a mass of evidence of the day, with television, radio and telephone communications recorded and preserved. On top of that, the *Insight* team of the *Sunday Times* conducted its own investigation in the weeks and months after 30 January 1972, which indicated that the armed forces were responsible for the untimely shootings.

Inevitably, much of this book focuses on the Bloody Sunday Inquiry; it seeks to explain why the Inquiry took so long to perform its task of elucidating the happenings of the day without transgressing the function of determining any criminal or civil liability on the part of any person. But equally important has been the book's advocacy for the Inquiries Act 2005 which, the select committee of the House of Lords declared in March 2014,[1] 'provides the right procedural framework for both

[1] para 215.

the chairman and counsel to the inquiry to conduct an inquiry efficiently, effectively and above all fairly'.

The author of this book concludes from a tentative initial analysis of the framework of the Inquiries Act 2005 that the prime removal of the role of lawyers representing various witnesses to the investigated event effectively transposes the element of judiciality from the public inquiry and puts in place a commission of inquiry as an outreach of public administration. The Act of 2005 replaces the rubric of legal power (it is 'sterile of legal effect', as courts have dubbed inquiries set up under the 1921 Act) and reposes on the commission of inquiry the essential principle of 'fairness'[2] as determining the conduct of the inquiry and its ensuing report. Procedural control by the sponsors of the public inquiry must not be confused with the substance of the inquiry.

Judges regard themselves as different actors in the governmental sense. And in one sense they are an elite cadre. They form the judicial arm of our tripartite government. Not irrationally, the public places the judges on a pedestal of public affairs, and accords them a special status on account of their judicial office. In that sense judges are certainly 'a class apart'. Their position is prestigious, influential and constitutionally protected; essentially, they perform their task as and when they are carrying out their forensic duties in accordance with their special oath of office. But, at least since the abandonment in the 1980s of the Kilmuir Protocol released them from limitations on their public image, they are public servants of the Crown when not sitting on the Bench, although inferentially they still bear a responsibility for their judicial behaviour and probably undergo relentless public scrutiny and expectation; the media are ever alert to judicial culture. In a modern democracy they no longer can claim 'cloistered virtues' for their decisions made in the courtroom. Some limitations imposed conventionally on judges include restrictions on their freedom to speak freely in public, even as far as criticising fellow judges for their decisions, in the instant case or otherwise. Some expression can even, exceptionally, be related to issues of social policy, exercised appropriately without descending to the degree of outright hostility, à la Scaliaism. (Scaliaism is a shorthand to depict the frontal attack by Justice Antonin Scalia on some other Justices of a liberal bent in the Supreme Court of the United States. Antonin Scalia was himself a notable jurist of rare distinction.) As and when the judge (serving or retired) accepts the ministerial request to conduct a public inquiry (whether statutory or under the prerogative power of the government) the judge is often capable of finding blameworthiness in any individual witness, subject of course to the requirement of fair treatment in providing warnings to witnesses to safeguard reasonably their reputation from serious harm that may ensue when the report is published by the minister. These changing conditions in a literate society render

---

[2] Inquiries Act 2005, s 17(3).

the extra-curricular judge a commissioner of inquiry as a species of conducting public affairs and elucidating the lessons of past public disasters and social scandals. The commission of inquiry is, as Lord Bingham propounded in 1993, 'unlike any court of law'; whatever else, it is public administration.

This book fastens on the insistence by Lord Saville on maintaining an outmoded practice of lawyers for a public inquiry in pursuance of proving individual culpability for the deaths of 13 innocent marchers on Bloody Sunday, instead of concentrating on the reasons why and how the tragedy happened. The latter, the author contends, was Saville's allotted task, and his failure to recognise and adhere to it resulted in unnecessary delay and public expense.

# 15

## Postscript—Lessons Learned, or Another Wrong Turn?

After two false starts for the Independent Child Sexual Abuse Inquiry (ICSA), which was to be non-statutory under its two designated chairmen, Lady Butler-Sloss and subsequently Lady Fiona Woolf, the Home Secretary appointed the New Zealand judge, Justice Dame Lowell Goddard as the chairman with four panel members[1] as an inquiry under the Inquiries Act 2005 (the publicity of Justice Goddard as chair of a statutory inquiry prompted the Home Secretary (Theresa May, since July 2016 the Prime Minister) to bring the inquiry under the Inquiries Act). Litvinenko was converted from a coroner's inquest to a public inquiry under the Act, seemingly only because his widow judicially reviewed the Home Secretary's power to refer it to a coroner's court, on the appointment of Sir Robert Owen, a retired High Court judge.

At a preliminary hearing on 9 July 2015, Justice Dame Lowell Goddard made an opening statement (30 pages long) setting out the methodology of the inquiry to be adopted, and indicating the various steps to be taken by the Inquiry. By any standards, it is an impressive document, and will serve as a model for future chairmen. Since this histological inquiry 'must also provide an enduring legacy for future generations'—Justice Goddard's own words—it will become the largest and most ambitious public inquiry ever established in England and Wales, its scope and purpose being too extensive for emulation, but with elements of it being prospectively informative and providing helpful analogies. Even the promise to issue interim reports is a welcome innovation. That is thankfully precedential. The opening statement of 9 July on the scale of the inquiry is a forward approach, with defined objectives from the outset and a working structure that is clear and predicted as extremely welcome as expressing the overall public interest in the inquiry.

In considerable anticipation, some tentative observations about the operation of 'core participants' in the third of the complementary methodologies of the inquiry's work—entitled 'public interests'—to hear the victims of sexual abuse is puzzling (paras 52–56). While each victim has a personal (and wider) interest, the statutory

---

[1] Professor Michael Evans, Ivor Frank, Professor Alexis Jay and Don Sharping.

entitlement to seek *core* participation seems primarily not to be applicable. Perhaps the premature mention of the provision for restricted legal representation is merely precautionary and not necessarily intended to be implemented. Parenthetically, is it accurate to describe (at para 62) the oral proceedings as 'judicial'? Surely, the taking of evidence, even if produced inquisitorially, is adduced as a method of testing the credibility and reliability of witnesses, obtained in a non-judicial forum; it is devoid of judicial power. The acquisition of evidential material is performed only in a court of law under strict rules of procedure. Only then can one talk of judicial power. On the irksome aspect of the consequences of the cost and delay of the inquiry's report there is mention of the Inquiry Rules 2006. There is, unhappily, no reference to their criticism by the House of Lords in the course of proceedings on rules 13–15, and their likely amendment.

The most notable explanation in the opening statement is the nature of the Inquiry's task in establishing the testimony of the witnesses. It states:

> 71. We know that for some people, engaging with the Inquiry will be a difficult process. We recognise that trauma, fear and shame can be major barriers to disclosure, and that for many people the painful memories of abuse will be retriggered by the process of discussing their experiences with someone from the Inquiry. The Australian Royal Commission, for example, found that it took an average of over 20 years for people who had been sexually abused in childhood to disclose this fact to a person in authority. Building trust, and enabling people to speak in an environment in which they feel safe, is a priority. We are very much aware that, for some people, coming forward to the Inquiry may be the first time they have ever disclosed. Even the fact that the Inquiry is taking place has caused some victims and survivors to experience anxiety and distress. The need to provide adequate support is therefore a paramount consideration.

> 72. To meet this need the Inquiry is securing specialist sexual violence advocates to provide advocacy and support to victims and survivors of abuse who choose to engage with the Inquiry.

The opening statement makes no specific reference to witnesses' memory of traumatic events, many of them experienced in their youth in care (and relived over the many years since), and the possibility of their invalidation (or at least, suspicion over their validity). On 4 August 2016 Justice Dame Lowell Goddard resigned: in her letter of resignation addressed to the Home Secretary, she gave no reasons. A fourth chairman—Professor Alexis Jay, a distinguished social worker, and an existing panel member—was appointed.

The disruption in September 2016 to the personnel of ICSA underlines how important it is to establish the precise terms of a public inquiry and the appropriate selection of the Commissioner(s) under the Inquiries Act 2005. Progress in the early days of ICSA has been slowed, in part, by the representatives of alleged victims of child abuse approaching those appointed to carry out the inquiry's task. It is important that, once the inquiry has been firmly set in motion by the sponsoring Minister, the Commissioner(s) and staff must be left to conduct the proceedings uninterrupted by any interested parties. Once any claimants have justifiably persuaded the government that public concern about the national disaster or scandal demands a public inquiry, they should step aside and not air their views; their loud voices should be reserved for the testimony they will be asked to give. Confidence in the inquiry is impaired if some alleged victims voice their views otherwise than as witnesses.

The second lesson to be learnt is the selection of the commissioner. There is the question of their expertise in appointing counsel to the inquiry. It is normal practice for a chairman from the judiciary to appoint as his or her counsel some-one from among the ranks of practising advocates, but even if the chairman is not a lawyer (the fourth appointee to ICSA, Alexis Jay, is a prominent social worker) there can be no harm in a selection from among practising lawyers as the inquiry's counsel. The aim must be to ensure that the commissioner conducts the inquiry in harmony, if not in harness, with the legal team that adduces the evidence of the witnesses and advises the inquiry on any dispute arising from inquiry issues.

The inquiry's remit to report on the terms of reference efficiently and expediously cannot easily survive in the face of difficulties such as those posed by the claimants in the ICSA investigation.

The threatened challenge in the courts to the appointment of Professor Jay as the fourth chairman for the inquiry should result authoritatively and unambiguously in a ruling on the precise status of a commission of inquiry under the Inquiries Act 2005 to explain the circumstances surrounding public disasters and social scandals. Given its remit on the historical and institutional abuse, the inquiry is inevitably about the system and services for child protection in times gone by, and the focus is on the material and oral evidence uncovered but still available to those involved institutionally on behalf of numerous, but unrevealed, victims of child abuse. Their testimony and their cases are the subject of memory of unpalatable events, often committed out of public sight or sound. Whatever the size of the task—admittedly, enormous—there is still every reason for informing the Home Secretary of the whys and wherefores of the official treatment of children, however incomplete and unremediable. The overriding interest must be that of the British public; not just those whose hurt from child abuse has not yet been recognised and which was ineffectively evaluated long ago. The outcome must contemplate inconclusiveness. But the time taken by the inquiry should be tolerated, to restore the public image of child protection.

Memory is a crucial element in seeking retrospectively the truth of previously uninvestigated or unreported events of a sexual nature. Might not the ravages of time, relevant to the fallacies of memory (in particular, to childhood experiences), be a strong factor for governments to conclude that 'enough is enough', such as to draw a line over the untoward events of the past? Governments need to review the uncovering of events, historically ventilated by oral testimony as well as documentary material. Periods of limitation are globally recognised. But it is time that they were reviewed.

# ANNEX 1: LIST OF INQUIRIES UNDER THE 1921 ACT

| No | Name of Inquiry | Tribunal Members | Year | Publication |
|----|-----------------|------------------|------|-------------|
| 1 | Destruction of documents by Ministry of Munitions Officials | Lords Cave and Inchape, Sir William Plender | 1921 | Cmd 1340 |
| 2 | Royal Commission on Lunacy and Mental Disorder | H Macmillan | 1924 | Cmd 2700 |
| 3 | Arrest of Major R O Sheppard | J Rawlinson | 1925 | Cmd 2497 |
| 4 | Allegations made against the Chief Constable of Kilmarnock | W Mackenzie | 1925 | Cmd 2659 |
| 5 | Conditions with regard to mining and drainage in an area around the County Borough of Doncaster | Sir H Munro | 1926–28 | |
| 6 | Charges against the Chief Constable of St Helens by the Watch Committee | C Parry, T Walker | 1928 | Cmd 3103 |
| 7 | Interrogation of Miss Irene Savidge by Metropolitan Police at New Scotland Yard | Sir JE Banks, H Lees-Smith, J Withers | 1928 | Cmd 3147 |
| 8 | Allegations of bribery and corruption in connection with the letting and allocation of stances and other premises under the control of the Corporation of Glasgow | Lord Anderson, Sir R Boothby, J Hunter | 1933 | Cmd 4361 |
| 9 | Unauthorised disclosure of information relating to the Budget | Sir J Porter, G Simonds, R Oliver | 1936 | Cmd 5184 |
| 10 | The circumstances surrounding the loss of HM Submarine *Thetis* | Sir J Bucknill | 1939 | Cmd 6190 |

(*Continued*)

| No | Name of Inquiry | Tribunal Members | Year | Publication |
|---|---|---|---|---|
| 11 | The conduct before the Hereford Juvenile Court Justices of the proceedings against Craddock and others | Lord Goddard | 1943 | Cmd 6485 |
| 12 | The administration of Newcastle-upon-Tyne Fire, Police and Civil Defence Services | R Burrows | 1944 | Cmd 6522 |
| 13 | Bribery of Ministers of the Crown or other public servants in connection with the grant of licences, etc | Sir J Lynskey, G Russel Vick, G Upjohn | 1948 | Cmd 7616 |
| 14 | Allegations of improper disclosure of information relating to the raising of the Bank Rate | Lord Parker, E Holland, G Veale | 1957 | Cmnd 350 |
| 15 | Allegations that John Waters was assaulted on 7 December 1957 at Thurso | Lord Sorn, Sir J Robertson | 1959 | Cmnd 718 |
| 16 | The circumstances in which offences under the Official Secrets Act were committed by William Vassall | Lord Radcliffe, Sir J Barry, Sir Milner Holland | 1962 | Cmnd 2009 |
| 17 | The circumstances surrounding the mining disaster at Aberfan on 21 October 1966 | Sir E Davies, H Harding, V Lawrence | 1967 | HC 553 |
| 18 | The events on Sunday, 30 January 1972 which led to loss of life in connection with the procession in Londonderry that day | Lord Widgery | 1972 | HC 220/72 |
| 19 | The circumstances leading to the cessation of trading by the Vehicle and General Ins Co Ltd | Sir A James, M Kerr, S Templeman | 1972 | HC 133 |
| 20 | The extent to which the Crown Agents lapsed from accepted standards of commercial or professional conduct or of public administration as financiers on their own account in the years 1967–74 | Sir D Croom-Johnson, Sir W Slimmings, Lord Allen | 1982 | HC 48 |

*(Continued)*

| No | Name of Inquiry | Tribunal Members | Year | Publication |
|----|-----------------|------------------|------|-------------|
| 21 | The shootings at Dunblane Primary School, 13 March 1996 | Lord Cullen | 1996 | HC 201 |
| 22 | Abuse of children in care in North Wales | Sir Ronald Waterhouse, M le Fleming, M Clough | 1996 | Cm 3386 |
| 23 | Harold Shipman Inquiry | Dame Janet Smith | 2005 | Cm 6394 |
| 24 | Bloody Sunday Inquiry | Lord Saville, Hon W Hoyt, Hon J L Toohey | 2010 | HC 29-I-HC 29-X, Vols 1-10 |

# ANNEX 2: EXTRACT FROM CRAMPTON v SECRETARY OF STATE FOR HEALTH (1993)

## Crampton and others v Secretary of State for Health

**COURT OF APPEAL (CIVIL DIVISION)**

**SIR THOMAS BINGHAM MR, STEYN, HOFFMANN LJJ**

**9 July 1993**

A Ullstein QC and J Southgate for the First Applicant; C Chruszcz QC and J Phillips for the Second Applicant; R Gordon for the Third Applicant; P Havers and J McManus for the Respondent

Alexander Harris, Cheshire; R Bernard, Director of Legal Services; Royal College of Nursing; Brian Thompson and Partners, Sheffield; Solicitor to the Department of Health

### SIR THOMAS BINGHAM MR

These are renewed applications for leave to move for judicial review. They arise out of the events which culminated in the conviction of Beverley Allitt by a jury of four counts of murder, three counts of attempted murder, and six counts of causing grievous bodily harm. She was sentenced to life imprisonment on each count. These are events which have touched the heart and aroused the conscience of the nation. That one professionally charged with care of the very young should have abused her position to inflict injury and even death on these vulnerable patients is in the most literal sense horrifying. Not surprisingly, the parents of the children who have suffered, the professional bodies most closely concerned, and also the public at large, have shown anxiety to learn how these disastrous events were allowed to occur and how any risk of repetition in the future can be obviated, not only in the area where Beverley Allitt worked but in the country as a whole. It is obvious that unless full and satisfactory answers to these questions are provided public confidence in hospital paediatric services may well be in jeopardy.

More specifically, these applications arise out of the decision of the Secretary of State for Health to appoint a non-statutory tribunal to inquire into these matters. Although the Secretary of State has power under s 84 of the National Health

Service Act 1977 to cause an inquiry to be held and any such inquiry will, under the section, be armed with power to compel the attendance of witnesses and the production of documents on pain of criminal penalty for non-compliance and to administer oaths, the Secretary of State has not sought (certainly she has not intended) to exercise her powers under that section. Instead she has caused the Trent Regional Health Authority to establish a non-statutory tribunal, lacking compulsory powers. Its members are Sir Cecil Clothier QC formerly the Parliamentary Commissioner (Ombudsman) and National Health Service Commissioner (Health Services Ombudsman), Professor David Shaw, the Emeritus Professor of Clinical Neurology at the University of Newcastle-Upon-Tyne and Anne McDonald, Director of Quality at the Royal Manchester Childrens Hospital.

Sir Cecil advised, no doubt relying upon his previous experience, that he did not think the inquiry would require compulsory powers to carry out a full and effective inquiry, but added that if he did require such powers he would approach the Secretary of State and ask her to confer them under s 84. She, for her part, has indicated that if such a request is made she will accede to it.

The three applicants are, effectively, the parents of one of the injured children, whom it is fair to regard as speaking for all the parents, the Royal College of Nursing, and the Confederation of Health Service Employees (whom I shall hereafter refer to as "COHSE"). No question has been raised as to the standing of the two latter bodies to apply and I do not for a moment doubt that they are motivated by a genuine concern for the interests of their members and the public at large. The focus of that concern is the inquiry's lack of compulsory powers, at least in the first instance. Complaint has also been made of Sir Cecil's announced intention that the inquiry will be conducted and hear evidence in private without public hearings and without multi-party representation. But this was advanced very much as a secondary complaint and understandably so, since even if the Secretary of State had established the inquiry under s 84, as it is said she should have done, the inquiry need not have been held in public. This may no doubt be the usual practice in inquiries established under s 84, and in many cases where it is sought to allay public concern it will be thought preferable to conduct the proceedings under the public eye, but the facts of different cases vary infinitely and had the Secretary of State established an inquiry under s 84 it would have been very hard, if possible at all, for the parties to challenge a decision made then or thereafter that the inquiry should not be held in public…

It was obvious to all at an early stage that some form of inquiry into these tragic events was called for and the sooner the better. But there was an obvious difficulty about doing anything public which could prejudice Beverley Allitt as a defendant pleading not guilty at a forthcoming criminal trial…

On 8 June 1993 the Secretary of State wrote to the General Secretary of the Royal College of Nursing and said:

> I am determined that the full truth about the tragic events at Grantham Hospital should be fully uncovered. All lessons should be learned from them and the necessary action taken in response. The Clothier inquiry is the best way of achieving this.

Sir Cecil's advice, based on long experience, is that the truth about this case is more likely to emerge through an independent investigative inquiry than in an adversarial public forum. He and his team are all of the utmost independence, integrity and expertise and I believe that we can have full confidence in their ability to establish the facts. Their findings and recommendations will be made public. It will be for them to determine the detailed proceedings of the inquiry. Everyone giving evidence to the inquiry is at liberty to make that evidence public...

The challenge to the Secretary of State's decision is put under three heads. First, it relates to her power to order such an inquiry as she did. Second, it relates to her failure to take account of relevant matters in reaching her decision. Thirdly, it relates to the rationality of her decision. It seems logical to begin with the question of power and I do so.

This argument was principally developed by Mr Gordon on behalf of COHSE and was adopted by the other parties. It was an argument of considerable sophistication and ingenuity and I fear I shall do it an injustice. It boiled down, I think, to a contention that the Secretary of State either caused this inquiry to be set under s 84 with the result that the statutory consequences in the shape of compulsory powers necessarily follow or that the inquiry was not validly and lawfully established at all. Mr Gordon submitted that the inquiry was not established under s 2 of the 1977 National Health Service Act because a general power to establish an inquiry under s 2 cannot co-exist alongside a specific power in s 84, because the Secretary of State never purported to exercise, or until this hearing claimed to have exercised, power under s 2, and because the terms of reference are wider in their terms than the Secretary of State's duty under s 1 of the 1977 National Health Service Act which the exercise of power in s 2 must serve to promote. Mr Gordon also submitted that the Secretary of State's action could not be justified as an exercise of prerogative power, as suggested on behalf of the Secretary of State, since a prerogative power cannot survive the enactment of a specific statutory power to which consequences are attached. The Secretary of State either exercised power under s 84, whether she intended to or not, with the result that a s 84 inquiry was established, or her instruction was invalid in law.

I have to say that for my part I find this argument wholly unpersuasive...

I turn, therefore, to the second head which alleges that the Secretary of State failed to take into account matters which she should have taken into account. A number of matters advanced in the skeleton arguments and in oral argument related to the procedure which Sir Cecil Clothier's inquiry would or should follow. I shall deal with these matters separately. For the moment I shall only touch on the non-procedural aspects.

It was argued, first, that it was clear from the evidence that the staff at the Hospital wanted a public inquiry as various letters, Press releases and applications have made clear. It was also suggested that the Secretary of State wrongly regarded a statutory inquiry as liable to cause strain and stress for the staff. To that suggestion there are in my judgment a number of answers. The Secretary of State was fully entitled to take the view that a statutory inquiry, particularly if held in public, was bound to cause strain and stress for the staff. Even if a s 84 inquiry had been established, of course, it need not have been in public which is what most of the correspondence was directed to achieving. It is plain from the correspondence read as a whole that the Secretary of State was fully alive to the concerns expressed to her but she had and gave reasons for her decision and it was a decision for her. I find no reason to infer that she exercised it on any improper ground.

Secondly, it is said that she failed to take account of the recommendations of the Royal Commission on Tribunals of Inquiry 1966, the Salmon Report, and in particular failed to take account of the six cardinal principles laid down in that report. Again, as it seems to me, there are a number of answers. The report was specifically drawn to the Secretary of State's attention. There is no ground for saying that she ignored it. As the terms of reference make clear, the Royal Commission was established to review the working of the Tribunals of Inquiry (Evidence) Act 1921 and the recommendations of the Commission were clearly directed to inquiries under that Act. Further, while the rationale of the six cardinal principles is undoubtedly sound and anyone conducting an inquiry of this kind is well advised to have regard to them, the Royal Commission Report itself has not been embodied in legislation and numerous inquiries have been conducted, and satisfactorily conducted, since 1966 without observing the letter of those principles...

I turn to the third heading of the irrationality, which to some extent overlaps with the heading I have just considered. It is said first that the Secretary of State wrongly regarded the interests of the Health Authority as paramount and gave its views more weight than those of the parents, the staff and others. That judgment is in my view contradicted by the facts, which show that the Secretary of State rejected the Health Authority's representation that there should not be an inquiry led by a Queen's Counsel and that she was alive to other considerations. The weight that she attached to different considerations was a matter for her and her alone...

It is said that in view of the seriousness of the questions raised the Secretary of State gave undue weight to the question of cost. To my mind the Secretary of State might well have been at fault had she treated cost as the only consideration but she cannot be said to have erred in considering cost to be a material consideration. It is an undoubted truth that a statutory inquiry conducted in public would last longer and cost more and the money so spent would of course otherwise be available for the care of patients. This was pre-eminently a matter for the judgment of the Secretary of State.

Next it is said that it was irrational of the Secretary of State not to confer statutory powers under s 84 since the powers need not be used unless there is call to use them and it would do no harm for the inquiry to have the power. That is a legitimate point of view. There is, however, an alternative point of view favoured by the Secretary of State that there was no point in conferring the powers unless it looked as if they would be needed and that there is a virtue in voluntariness. That may or may not be agreed but it is to my mind an equally valid view-point.

Next it is said that Sir Cecil Clothier's reasons for favouring an inquisitorial form of inquiry as opposed to an adversarial procedure challenge the accepted wisdom underlying the British legal system. That is in my view a gross over-simplification. *It does not follow that the procedures suitable for inter-partes litigation or criminal prosecution are by any means necessarily appropriate for a fact finding exercise intended to result in management recommendations, a task quite unlike that which is entrusted to a court of law...*[1]

I turn, therefore, to the question of procedure. In this respect it is said that the procedure which is proposed is defective for a number of reasons. The inquiry will have to act as detective, inquisitor, advocate and judge. Parties subject to criticism, whether they be management, staff or employees within the Hospital, must, it is said, have the opportunity to hear the evidence, to cross-examine and to make submissions. Witnesses, it is pointed out, may be unwilling to give evidence if they are not afforded this protection. The parents will be unable to be represented throughout the hearings and will not be reimbursed save for the costs of their own appearances. The parties will not be alerted to the need to seek advice or protection in advance and will not know what if any case is made against them. Lastly, it is said that there will be no full record of all the evidence which will be made available to the public.

It is necessary first of all to remind oneself that this challenge by way of judicial review is directed to the Secretary of State's decision, not to the procedure which the inquiry either has adopted or may adopt, which is not the subject of these applications. There is a broader and more important point. It is necessary to remind oneself of the objects of the inquiry, which are to ensure that the facts are fully investigated and all relevant lessons learned, that all necessary changes are made and that public confidence in the paediatric services of this and other hospitals is restored in Lincolnshire and elsewhere. To that end it is essential that the inquiry should be searching, thorough and completely independent. It is essential that it should be conducted fairly. It is very highly desirable that the inquiry should be concluded as soon as reasonably possible consistent with the duty of full and fair investigation. It is highly desirable that the inquiry should not cost more than reasonably necessary to ensure a full and fair investigation. It is lastly essential that the inquiry should culminate in a full, fair, fearless, independent and objective report covering all matters falling within the terms of reference.

The procedural concerns which have been raised relate to the second of these aims. To allay those concerns Sir Cecil Clothier has now indicated that witnesses will be informed in advance of the areas the inquiry wish to cover with them; that points of potential criticism will be put to witnesses whether at an initial hearing or subsequently and witnesses will be given a full opportunity to respond; and that those likely to be criticised in the report will be given the opportunity to see

---

[1] Italics supplied.

that part of the report which relates to them and to respond to it before the report is submitted. The inquiry has already indicated that witnesses may be accompanied by a friend or legal advisor during their attendance and it is quite obvious that the inquiry will be vastly assisted by any representations which any relevant professional body may make either as to the present or as to recommendations for the future. It is said that some of these procedures were not followed with witnesses who testified earlier this week. The court has no specific information on that matter, which is in any event not relevant to these applications. No doubt, however, the inquiry will wish to publicise its proposed procedure and thereafter follow it. Precedents are available. I have no doubt that the inquiry will wish to be scrupulously fair. In the end, the effectiveness of an inquiry of this kind depends not on the procedure adopted but on the integrity, energy, skill and fairness of the tribunal and particularly the chairman. They and he will wish their inquiry to meet the highest standards, not only as a matter of professional duty, and not only out of concern for the public interest, but also and at the lowest because their own standing and reputation will be affected by the outcome.

I very much hope that the concerns aired at this hearing have now been in large measure alleviated and that all concerned will now do their utmost to enable the inquiry to discharge with complete success the difficult, sensitive and vitally important job it was established to do.

Although I would for my part refuse these applications I feel that they have served a useful purpose in illuminating the way ahead.

Lords Justices Steyn and Hoffmann agreed with the Master of the Rolls.

*Note* The refusal to consider the applications for judicial review was heard on 9 July 1993 and judgment, of ten pages of transcript, was given, unreserved. To the author's knowledge, the case has never been cited by subsequent courts.

# ANNEX 3: SIR JOHN CHILCOT'S WITNESS PROTOCOL IN 2009

## Protocol: Witnesses Giving Evidence to the Inquiry

This protocol addresses:

— what the Iraq Inquiry will expect from witnesses giving evidence to the Inquiry; and
— what witnesses may expect from the Inquiry and its Secretariat.

## Aims

1. This protocol is designed to ensure that:

a   the Inquiry gets the evidence that it needs to establish a reliable account of what happened between 2001 and the end of July 2009, and to identify the lessons that can be learned;
b   witnesses are aware how the Inquiry intends to work, how the evidence sessions will be managed, and whether they may expect to be identified and to give evidence in public;
c   witnesses have confidence that they will be treated fairly and with consideration;
d   the public have confidence that evidence to the Inquiry is given in public, and witnesses identified, except where there are genuine reasons not to; and
e   information will be properly protected if its publication would damage national security.

## Principles

2. The Iraq Inquiry is committed to ensuring that its proceedings are as open as possible. It recognises this is one of the ways in which the public can have confidence in the integrity and independence of the Inquiry process.

3. As much as possible of the Inquiry's hearings will therefore be in public. But for witnesses to be able to provide the evidence needed to get to the heart of what happened, and what lessons need to be learned for the future, some evidence

sessions will need to be private. That will be appropriate for example when it is necessary:

a to protect national security, international relations, or defence or economic interests;

b to ensure witnesses' welfare, personal security or freedom to speak frankly.

## Before the Session

4. The Inquiry will decide who it wants to invite to give written and/or oral evidence. That may be as a result of an approach to the Inquiry by the individual concerned, or at the Inquiry's own discretion. The Inquiry welcomes approaches from any individual who believes he/she has relevant information to offer. The Inquiry cannot however undertake to hear evidence from every person who puts his/her name forward.

5. The Inquiry may decide to hear certain evidence in private, and not to identify certain witnesses—see Protocol for hearing evidence by the Iraq Inquiry in public, and for identifying witnesses.

6. The Inquiry Secretariat will generally write 7 weeks in advance to any person who the Inquiry expects to invite as a witness. For serving and former Ministers, civil servants and Crown servants (including military personnel), the letters will normally be copied to relevant departments/agencies. The Secretariat will set out the broad areas where the Inquiry believes the witness can offer evidence, and invite the witness (and his/her department where relevant) to:

a identify dates when he/she would be unable to attend;

b if necessary, give reasons why some or all of the witness's evidence should be heard in private;

c where either the witness has requested a private hearing or the Inquiry has decided to invite the witness to give evidence in private, indicate whether or not the witness is content for authorised representatives of the relevant government department to be present during the hearing;

d if necessary, give reasons why the witness's identity should not be revealed in public; and

e make any other requests he/she wishes the Inquiry to consider.

7. The Secretariat will provide each witness, and his/her department where relevant, generally four weeks before the date of the session, with:

a the date, time and place of the session, and its expected duration;

b whether it will be in public or in private;

c if public, the extent to which it is proposed to broadcast the session;

d if a private session was requested but the Committee has decided to hear all or part of the evidence in public, the reasons behind that decision;

e  if the witness has asked not to be identified, but the Inquiry disagrees, the reasons (see further below);

f  an indication of the matters which the Inquiry wishes to cover during the session; and

g  documents the Inquiry wishes to refer to in the session (which will normally be limited to documents which the witness would have had access to at the time).

8. The Inquiry may also invite a witness to provide a written statement in advance of the witness session. The witness may in any case provide a written statement if he/she wishes. All such statements relating to public evidence sessions will be treated as publishable unless reasons are given why they should not be published. In case of disagreement the process given in Documents and other Written and Electronic Information will be followed, or an equivalent process where confidences belonging to parties outside HMG are at issue. Statements should be sent to the Secretariat (at 35 Great Smith Street, London SW1P 3BQ) to arrive at least one week before the date of the session.

9. If any of the detail provided at this stage causes the witness difficulty (for example if it exposes new matters that should not be discussed in public), if the witness does not understand the matters on which evidence is required or does not feel qualified to give evidence on them, or if the witness wishes to bring to the Inquiry's attention any documents he/she would wish to refer to, the witness should contact the Secretariat as soon as possible.

10. The prime purpose of the Inquiry is to identify lessons to be learned. The inquiry is not a court of law and nobody will be on trial, although the committee will not shy away from making criticisms if warranted. In the event that a particular witness may be the subject of criticism by the Inquiry, the Inquiry Secretariat will, in accordance with normal practice, notify that witness separately, in writing at least seven days in advance of the evidence session, of the nature of the potential criticism and the evidence that supports it.

11. Departments will if appropriate provide legal and welfare support for current and former Ministers, civil servants and Crown servants (including military personnel), to help them prepare any statements and to provide assistance in advance of hearings. Other categories of witnesses may wish to seek similar support; the Inquiry will look sympathetically at the costs of this support, and can recommend that they be met by the public purse.

## Requests for anonymity

12. If the witness has asked not to be identified, the Inquiry will consider the request applying the guidance in paragraph 4 of the Protocol for hearing evidence by the Iraq Inquiry in public, and for identifying witnesses. Requests from

witnesses falling into the categories outlined in 4 a) and b) of that Protocol are unlikely to be refused. If a witness seeks anonymity on other grounds, the Inquiry will consider the request on its merits applying the principles set out above and in that Protocol.

## At the Session

13. Evidence sessions will be conducted by the Privy Counsellors who make up the Inquiry Committee. They will be supported by members of the Inquiry Secretariat, and in some instances also by specialist advisers helping the Inquiry. Public sessions may be attended by the media and members of the public, and may be broadcast on television or radio, or streamed on the internet. The Inquiry will agree protocols with broadcasters, based on those adopted by Parliamentary Select Committees. Private sessions may be attended by an authorised representative of the relevant government department, unless the witness has requested otherwise.

14. Members of the Committee will question the witness. Questions from other people present will not be permitted. There will be no cross examination by lawyers acting on behalf of the Inquiry or of other parties. Witnesses should feel free to ask for explanation if they are not sure what the Inquiry wants from them.

15. The Inquiry recognises that particular questions may lead unexpectedly into sensitive matters that cannot be discussed in public. Witnesses should feel free to draw the Inquiry's attention to this. If the Inquiry judges that a matter should not be discussed in public, any further questioning on that will be deferred to a private session. If the Inquiry remains of the view that questioning should proceed in public, it shall resolve the matter through the process set out in Documents and Other Written and Electronic Information.

16. Witnesses may wish to be accompanied at hearings, for example by a friend, colleague, counsellor, trade union representative or legal adviser. Witnesses will be allowed one person to accompany them, who may sit close to them during hearings. In private sessions, this may be subject to the person having appropriate security clearance. In public sessions, other friends and colleagues may of course attend as members of the public. If a witness wishes for any reason to be accompanied when giving evidence, he/she should so request, ideally when first invited to give evidence (paragraph 6 above). The Inquiry will consider all such requests sympathetically.

17. During the hearing, a person (including a legal adviser) accompanying a witness will not be permitted to address the Inquiry Committee or speak on behalf of witnesses. Communication between the witness and the person accompanying him/her is not forbidden, but the Committee would expect that to be the exception; and that it should not disrupt the hearing or hinder the conduct of business.

# After the Session

## Transcripts

18. Draft transcripts of evidence will be provided to witnesses on the day of the session or the working day following. In the case of private hearings, the transcripts will be made available to the witness at the Inquiry's offices.

19. Witnesses will be invited to identify transcription errors, within a deadline of 5.00 pm on the working day following a public session or two working weeks following a private session (the difference in timescales reflecting the need for the witness to attend the Inquiry's offices to check the transcripts of private hearings).

20. Suggestions for "improving" evidence will not be accepted. If witnesses wish to correct their evidence, they may submit an addendum for consideration by the Committee. Witnesses will be asked to sign a statement confirming that their evidence as transcribed and corrected is truthful, fair and accurate.

# Publication

21. In respect of public hearings, a draft transcript—marked as 'uncorrected'—will be placed on the Inquiry's website at the time the text is sent to the witness for checking. This will be replaced by the final transcript once the witness has signed the statement confirming that the evidence, as transcribed, is truthful, fair and accurate.

22. As explained in the Protocol for hearing evidence in Public and for identifying witnesses, the Committee will give careful consideration to how best to draw on and explain in public what was covered in a private session, either in its final Report or at an earlier stage—for example, in the general interests of transparency or to pursue a point with a future witness in public session. This could be done in a range of ways, for example:

a   an unclassified summary of the nature of the evidence taken during the private hearing (this approach may be likely where the sensitivity of the evidence is such that it would not be possible to redact the transcript without rendering it unintelligible, but where the Committee nevertheless believes it is important, in the interests of transparency, to make clear the nature of the hearing);

b   a redacted transcript of the evidence (this approach could be adopted where it is possible to redact sensitive sections of a transcript without affecting the overall its comprehensibility; or

c   a full transcript (this approach is only likely to be possible where a private hearing has been held because of, for example, welfare concerns for a junior member of staff but where the nature of the evidence itself is not sensitive).

23. The Inquiry will apply the Protocol between the Iraq Inquiry and HMG regarding Documents and Other Written and Electronic Information to ensure that evidence relating to classified documents and/or sensitive matters (within the terms of the Protocol on Sensitive Information) is not inappropriately disclosed;

24. In addition, in cases where the Inquiry wishes to publish a summary of the nature of evidence taken rather than a full transcript, it will confirm with the witness that the text proposed for publication is an accurate reflection of the relevant part(s) of their evidence. In cases where the Inquiry has granted anonymity to a witness, it will confirm with the witness that the text proposed for publication does not contain any information that would reveal their identity.

25. If evidence is given during a private hearing which neither relates to classified documents nor engages any of the categories set out in the Protocol on Sensitive Information, that evidence would be capable of being published, subject to the process outlined above.

26. The transcript of a private hearing—other than any redacted version of it which is published—will remain the property of the Inquiry and will be accessible only by the Inquiry, the witness and, where appropriate, the authorised representative of the relevant department(s)

27. Witnesses will not routinely be provided with transcripts of the evidence given in private hearings by other witnesses where they cover similar subject matter. However, in the interests of fairness, where a witness gives evidence which is potentially adverse to or critical of another witness, the Inquiry will disclose relevant extracts of that evidence to the witness in order to permit him or her to respond to it. Where necessary and appropriate, the identity of the maker of the adverse comment may be disclosed. Disclosure will be effected by the witness viewing the relevant part of the transcript at the Inquiry's offices.

## Further evidence

28. Any witness who wishes to give further evidence should contact the Secretariat. The Inquiry will consider such requests carefully. If the Inquiry wishes to recall a witness, the Secretariat will provide appropriate notice.

## Expenses

29. Witnesses who are serving or former Ministers, civil servants or Crown servants (including military personnel) should contact their departments for payment of expenses. In other cases the Inquiry will pay reasonable travel and accommodation expenses of witnesses.

## The Inquiry Report

30. If the Inquiry expects to criticise an individual in the final report, that individual will, in accordance with normal practice, be provided with relevant sections of the draft report in order to make any representations on the proposed criticism prior to publication of the final report.

# INDEX

www.ingramcontent.com/pod-product-compliance
Lightning Source LLC
Chambersburg PA
CBHW062034270326
41929CB00014B/2423